T0275653

# Online Social Networks: Human Cognitive Constraints in Facebook and Twitter Personal Graphs

# Online Social Networks: Human Cognitive Constraints in Facebook and Twitter Personal Graphs

Valerio Arnaboldi

Andrea Passarella

Marco Conti

Robin I.M. Dunbar

ELSEVIER

AMSTERDAM • BOSTON • HEIDELBERG • LONDON • NEW YORK • OXFORD
PARIS • SAN DIEGO • SAN FRANCISCO • SINGAPORE • SYDNEY • TOKYO

Elsevier
Radarweg 29, PO Box 211, 1000 AE Amsterdam, Netherlands
The Boulevard, Langford Lane, Kidlington, Oxford OX5 1GB, UK
225 Wyman Street, Waltham, MA 02451, USA

**Notices**

Knowledge and best practice in this field are constantly changing. As new research and experience
broaden our understanding, changes in research methods, professional practices, or medical treatment
may become necessary.

Practitioners and researchers must always rely on their own experience and knowledge in evaluating
and using any information, methods, compounds, or experiments described herein. In using such
information or methods they should be mindful of their own safety and the safety of others, including
parties for whom they have a professional responsibility.

To the fullest extent of the law, neither the Publisher nor the authors, contributors, or editors, assume
any liability for any injury and/or damage to persons or property as a matter of products liability,
negligence or otherwise, or from any use or operation of any methods, products, instructions, or ideas
contained in the material herein.

**Library of Congress Cataloging-in-Publication Data**
A catalog record for this book is available from the Library of Congress

**British Library Cataloguing in Publication Data**
A catalogue record for this book is available from the British Library

ISBN: 978-0-12-803023-3

# CONTENTS

# PREFACE

Online social networks (OSNs), like Facebook and Twitter, are undoubtedly changing the way we communicate and manage our social lives. The ability to access OSNs from our smart mobile devices is contributing to the so-called cyber-physical world (CPW) convergence, which envisions a world where virtual and physical social interactions are often indistinguishable and completely dependent upon each other.

In this scenario, the analysis of OSNs is a very intriguing and important topic for two reasons. One is that analysing the behaviour of OSN users can lead to new insights into human social behaviour. Whilst it is known that people's social capacity is bounded by their limited cognitive and time resources, the effect of OSNs on these limits is still not completely understood. The other is that OSNs are one of the primary means of communication between users and information access in the CPW. Understanding the key features of human relationships inside OSNs may thus help in designing novel user-centric services.

In this book, we investigate these aspects, presenting a series of analyses on the structural properties of personal social network graphs (known as *ego networks*) in Facebook and Twitter. The book uses a multidisciplinary approach to the study of social networks, discussing the most recent advances in the field. The results presented in this book indicate that ego networks in Facebook and Twitter show the same structural properties as those found by previous studies in offline environments (not mediated by OSNs). This suggests that, despite having initiated a radical change in our lives, OSNs may be unable to improve our social capacity, because that, apparently, remains constrained by the limited nature of the capacities of our brain. Moreover, thanks to the analysis of the large volume of data available from Facebook and Twitter, it has been possible to find also original results in terms of new properties on the structure of ego networks that were not visible in offline social networks. This suggests that we can use the study of large-scale online communication datasets to deepen knowledge about human social behaviour. In effect, online data represent a sort of social microscope to investigate human behaviour.

Finally, in the book, we discuss how OSN structural properties could be exploited to extend social network analysis, and to create future online services. We discuss several such examples, including the analysis of information diffusion, and we also present initial results on new communication platforms based on the concepts discussed in this book, showing how the highlighted OSN structural properties impact on key features of this type of services.

# ACKNOWLEDGEMENTS

Valerio Arnaboldi would like to thank his family for their support during the book-writing process.

Marco Conti wishes to thank his wife, Laura, for her invaluable support understanding and inspiration, throughout this book project, and in everyday life.

Andrea Passarella expresses his gratitude to Erica, his wife, for her constant understanding, encouragement and for being such a great life partner.

The work for this book of Valerio Arnaboldi, Marco Conti and Andrea Passarella has been carried out also in the European Laboratory on Big Data Analytics and Social Mining (SoBigData, http://www.sobigdata.eu), a joint laboratory involving IIT-CNR and a number of other institutions active in the area of Social Mining. SoBigData is leading, under H2020, the SoBig-Data Research Infrastructure, the only EU-funded Research Infrastructure on BigData and social data mining.

Robin I.M. Dunbar's research is supported by a European Research Council Advanced grant.

# CHAPTER 1

# Introduction

## 1.1 OFFLINE AND ONLINE SOCIAL NETWORKS

In its classical definition, a 'social network' represents a social structure containing a set of actors and a set of dyadic ties identifying social relationships existing between these actors in the considered social context (e.g. a workplace, a country, the scientific community) [1]. Social network analysis is aimed at understanding social phenomena arising in the contexts in question (e.g. the circulation of new ideas in a workplace, the spread of diseases or the creation of collaborations among scientists) by looking at structural properties of these networks.

The recent advent of social media, like Facebook and Twitter, is creating new opportunities for the analysis of social networks. In fact, some social media are now so widely used that they can represent a large portion of an individual's entire social world, and their analysis could therefore provide new insights into our social behaviour. In contrast to more traditional means of communication (such as face-to-face interaction or communication by phone), social media are gradually generating a completely new 'online' social environment, where social relationships do not necessarily map pre-existing relationships established face-to-face, but can also be created and maintained only in the virtual world. To highlight the differences between these social environments, we define 'online' social networks (hereinafter OSNs) as the social networks formed of users of specific social media and the social links existing between them, and 'offline' social networks as all the other social networks not mediated by the use of social media (e.g. networks formed through face-to-face interactions and phone calls). Our definition of OSNs emphasises the capacity that social media offer for projecting ourselves in the virtual world of online communications, something that other communication services are not able to do. This distinction between 'online' and 'offline' social networks will be extensively used in this book to analyse and discuss the differences between the social environments they embody.

Facebook and Twitter surely represent nowadays the most important and the largest OSNs in the world, and they will be the main subject of discussion in this book. For the readers who are less familiar with them, we give a brief description of their main features, introducing the terms that we shall encounter in the rest of the book.

*Facebook* is the most used online social networking service in the world, with more than 1.3 billion monthly active users as of the first quarter of 2015 [2]. It was founded in 2004 and is open to everyone over 13 years old. Facebook provides several features for social interaction. Users have a *profile* which reports their personal information, and can be customised. Connected to their profile, users have a special message board called *wall*, which reports all the status messages they create (*status updates*) as well as messages received from other users (*posts*). Posts can contain multimedia information such as pictures, URLs and videos. Users can *comment* on posts to create discussions with other users or to add information to them. To be able to communicate with another user (e.g. writing posts on her wall and commenting on her posts or photos), a user must obtain her *friendship*. A friendship is a bi-directional relation that requires the acceptance of the involved users. Users can visualise a summary of the activity of their *friends* through a special page called a *news feed*. This page presents real-time notifications describing the activities performed by friends, including posts and the comments they create, photos they add, etc. Direct communication between Facebook users is provided through posts, which can be written on the wall of other users. Posts can also contain references to multiple users. Private communications are provided by a chat called *messenger*. Facebook also provides other mechanisms to communicate online, such as voice and video calls. A widely used feature of Facebook is the *like* button, which allows people to express their favourable opinion about contents (e.g. posts, pictures).

*Twitter* is an online social networking and microblogging service founded in 2006, with roughly 300 million monthly active users as of the second quarter of 2014 [3]. In Twitter, users can post short messages (with at most 140 characters) called *tweets*. Users can automatically receive notifications of new tweets created by other users by 'following' them (i.e. creating a subscription to their notifications). People following a user are called her *followers*, whilst the set of people followed by the user are her *friends*.

Tweets can be enriched with multimedia content (i.e. URLs, videos and pictures) and by some special marks. Specifically, a tweet can reference one or more users with a special mark called a *mention*. Users mentioned in a tweet automatically receive a notification, even though they are not followers of the tweet's author. Users can also *reply* to tweets. In this case, a tweet is generated with an implicit mention to the author of the replied tweet.

In Twitter, users can *retweet* tweets, or, in other words, forward tweets to all their followers. Each tweet can be assigned to a topic through the use of a special character called hashtag (i.e. '#') placed before the text indicating the topic. Hashtags are used by Twitter to classify the tweets and to obtain *trending topics*, which can be visualised and searched for through a special page. A *trending topic* is a word, phrase or topic that begins to be mentioned at unusually high frequencies.

## 1.2 OSNs IN THE CYBER-PHYSICAL CONVERGENCE SCENARIO

Without any doubt, OSNs, like Facebook and Twitter, have deeply changed the way people interact with each other, from teenagers to older folks. Perhaps more surprisingly, the cultural change they have enacted is going far beyond a simple mutation in the way we express ourselves and communicate. Every action which involves a social interaction can now be done through OSNs, such as looking for a new job, advertising something, or organising events, just to mention a few examples. In addition, we have access to OSNs potentially from everywhere, and all the time, thanks to the smart mobile devices in our pockets.

The use of mobile and pervasive devices is affecting the development of our ecosystems, by constantly interlinking the cyber and the physical realities in which we are immersed. Information related to the physical world is captured through mobile devices, and then transferred to the cyber world, affecting the state of virtual applications and services, which, in turn, can modify or adapt the physical world around us through actuators. This is contributing to a gradual convergence toward a cyber-physical world (CPW) [4]. This convergence is paving the way for the creation of innovative applications, which, by exploiting the physical and the social contexts of their users, can improve services in the cyber world.

In a converged CPW, physical events and actions affecting the personal and social spheres of users influence the way information is handled in the cyber world. Humans are at the core of this process, as, through the use of smart devices, they capture aspects of physical events by creating content (e.g. pictures, videos, text) and transferring them to the cyber world. Social media provide a powerful way of performing these actions, supporting a user-centric communication paradigm whereby people actively contribute to the creation and diffusion of information, influenced by the social structures that exist in our society. This places OSNs at the core of the CPW scenario. The analysis of OSNs is important for two main reasons. On the one hand, it is useful for understanding human social behaviour in a new virtual environment, and the social phenomena arising in this environment. On the other hand, it can help to create new human-centric services and applications which exploit the knowledge acquired from the study of OSNs.

As an example of how the study of OSN structures can be useful for understanding online social phenomena, we can consider the impact that OSNs are already having on information diffusion. Studies conducted hitherto on the global structure of OSNs indicate that they show typical properties of 'small-world networks', with short average distance between users, and high clustering coefficient. Moreover, OSNs show long-tailed distributions of the number of social connections per user (i.e. most people regularly contact only a few individuals, but a small number of people have a very large number of contacts). In addition, almost every user is reachable from all the other parts of the network, thus forming a connected 'giant component'. This results in a very favourable condition for the diffusion of information, and is placing OSNs amongst the preferred communication channels for advertising, rapidly replacing traditional means such as the television and the radio. Despite these results, designing human-centred services by exploiting OSN structural properties is still in its infancy, and many more areas can be foreseen where this approach will be exploited.

In addition, from the standpoint of OSN analysis, significant effort has been put to analyse global properties of OSNs (which we shall describe in more detail in the rest of the book). However, from the standpoint of individuals, we still do not have a clear view of the effects of the use of OSNs on the structure of our personal social networks, and on our capacity for handling social relationships. Undoubtedly, OSNs are powerful means in that they allow us to connect, for example, with old classmates, or friends from overseas – individuals whom it would be too expensive to contact using other more conventional communication means. What is more difficult to assess is whether OSNs are also improving our social capacity, perhaps by increasing the total number of relationships we can actively maintain. It could be that OSNs simply represent another tool for maintaining our social relationships, one that is certainly very useful but perhaps not able to deeply alter the structure of our social system, due to cognitive or other constraints on our behaviour. A natural starting point, then, for the investigation of this is the analysis of the structural properties of personal social networks of OSN users, called *egocentric networks* or simply *ego networks*.

## 1.3 EGO NETWORKS ANALYSIS AND THE SOCIAL BRAIN HYPOTHESIS

Ego networks govern the relationships between a user (ego) and her social peers (alters) and are therefore one of the fundamental building blocks that determine social behaviour in any type of human social network. In offline environments (outside OSNs), it has been found that the structural properties of ego networks are highly constrained. Specifically, our social capacity is bounded by a combination of the size of the human brain and of the limited time that can be allocated for the management of social relationships. These findings constitute the basis of the social brain hypothesis (SBH), which identifies the causes of brain evolution in the increasing 'computational' demands of social systems – i.e. on the fact that humans had to build larger and larger social networks as a key strategy of their evolutionary path, and that this required more 'computational resources' and thus bigger brains [5]. This hypothesis is in contrast with conventional wisdom over the past centuries, which assumed that the brain evolved to cope only (or mainly) with ecological problem-solving tasks such as how to make tools. The SBH, as opposed to other hypotheses, is able to explain why humans maintain such an expensive brain, which consumes about 20% of their total daily energy intake. Animals showing complex social processes such as tactical deception and coalition formation also have large brains, although the real driver for brain size seems to be the evolution on bonded social relationships based on closely intimate social relationships [6, 7]. This is particularly true for the neocortex, the part of the brain associated with reasoning and consciousness. Evidence of the SBH is provided by findings on primates, which highlight a correlation between neocortex size and social group size, a proxy of social system's complexity, as well as various aspects of social behaviour [8].

In human ego networks, social relationships are not 'flat', in the sense that their importance is not evenly distributed among alters. On the contrary, the internal structure of ego networks show a series of nested sub-networks in which the strength of social relationships, as in large-scale social networks, follows a long-tailed distribution. This generates a series of recognisable concentric circles of alters around individuals, coinciding with these sub-networks. These circles (or layers) are explained by the SBH as the formation of a series of alliances to maintain cohesion and stability in the social groups.

## 1.4 AIM OF THE BOOK

Even though OSNs have been largely studied in the literature, there are still no detailed results on the structural properties of online ego networks. The analysis of such properties could reveal important aspects of OSNs, and of human social behaviour in general. In fact, if online ego networks showed the same properties found by previous studies of offline social networks, this would indicate that they are controlled by the same cognitive and time constraints governing the offline world. In essence, although OSNs allow us to establish and maintain a potentially infinite number of connections, the effective number of relationships that we actively maintain could still be limited, as in other environments, due to our constrained nature. If this was true, we would be able to better predict how OSNs will evolve, and how people will behave. This is, of course, of great importance for the creation of novel online services.

This book presents extensive analyses on the structural properties of ego networks in Facebook and Twitter. These analyses have a double aim. On the one hand, we aim to provide a detailed analysis of ego networks in OSNs. This allows us to check whether or not OSNs radically change the structures found offline, and thus test the SBH in a completely different social environment. On the other hand, we want to provide understanding of human social behaviour in OSNs as guide to the optimisation of novel services based on OSNs.

The book also provides a brief but complete review of the most recent methods in social networks and ego networks analysis. We think that this could provide a useful source for students and researchers approaching the analysis of social networks from a multidisciplinary perspective, bringing together aspects of social networks which remained disjointed until now.

## 1.5 BOOK STRUCTURE

The book starts with a review of the most recent advances in the social network literature, reported in Chapter 2. This chapter provides the reader with the needed tools for a correct understanding of the analyses presented in the following chapters, and motivates the need for novel studies on online ego networks. Then, we present our contribution in the field, reporting the results extracted from our most recent publications, which relate to the structural analysis of ego networks in Facebook (Chapter 3) and Twitter (Chapter 4), respectively. In Chapter 5, we examine the evolutionary dynamics of social networks over a longer time scale within a Twitter environment, in order to study the growth and decay of relationships in more detail. Finally, in Chapter 6, we summarise the results presented in the book, and discuss how these results could be exploited to improve online services and create the bases for novel analyses on social networks.

# CHAPTER *2*

# Human Social Networks

## 2.1 INTRODUCTION

This chapter presents an overview of the main characteristics of social networks, and how they have been studied. It is organised in terms of two main axes: (i) the level of the analysis, which can be *macroscopic* (i.e. on complete social networks) or *microscopic* (i.e. on social links of individuals), and (ii) whether or not the importance of social relationships (the tie strength) is taken into account.

Macroscopic analyses seek to understand the global properties of the whole structure of social networks. They use indices that capture these properties without the need to analyse the details of each and every node in the network, as that is often unfeasible when there are a large number of elements in the network.

Microscopic studies are aimed at characterising social networks from the perspective of a single individual, considering only the portion of network formed of the set of relationships of that individual. These personal social networks are also called ego (or egocentric) networks. Ego networks are studied so as to understand social differences at the personal and relational level.

On the second axis, the analysis of tie strength permits us to refine the results found on social networks by considering differences in the importance of social links. Specifically, social networks can be presented as weighted or unweighted, where the former refers to the fact that weight of the tie reflects the level of interaction between any pair of nodes and the latter refers to the fact that the 'weight' of the tie is considered only to be all-or-none. Graphs weighted by the level of interaction between nodes are called 'interaction graphs', whilst unweighted social network graphs are called 'social graphs'. In microscopic studies, the tie strength has a fundamental role since it permits us to differentiate single social relationships, the building blocks of ego networks. For this reason, in the literature there are only a few examples of microscopic analyses on unweighted ego networks, and in this book we present only analyses on weighted ego network graphs.

After we have discussed this classification in more detail, the chapter is divided into four sections. Section 2.2 presents the key properties of social networks from a macroscopic point of view, considering the networks as unweighted graphs. Macroscopic studies typically use tools derived from graph theory and complex networks analysis, which are described in Section 2.2.1. Section 2.2.2 presents in detail the fundamental macroscopic properties found through the analysis of unweighted social networks. Based on these features, a series of models for the generation of synthetic social network graphs have been proposed in the literature (see Section 2.2.3). In Section 2.3, we present the main results found through macroscopic analyses of interaction graphs. Then, Section 2.4 presents the main properties of ego networks found through microscopic analyses. Finally, Section 2.5 presents studies aimed at bridging the gap between macroscopic studies of social network graphs and microscopic analyses of behavioural and social aspects of ego networks, which we identify as meso-level analyses.

## 2.2 MACROSCOPIC PROPERTIES OF UNWEIGHTED SOCIAL NETWORKS

### 2.2.1 Complex Network Indices

Complex network analysis is a very extensive topic of research in statistical physics. Interested readers are referred to [9, 10] for more details.

In macroscopic analyses, the social network, such as the very simple one depicted in Figure 2.1, is seen as a unique global graph. Complex network methods have been designed to analyse exactly this type of network, and therefore they are often applied to macroscopic analyses of social networks. Specifically, in these cases, social networks are expressed in the form of a graph $G(V, E)$, where a vertex (or node) $x \in V$ represents a social actor, and the set of edges (or links) $E$ contains pairs of elements $(x, y)$ representing the social relationship between $x$ and $y$. Social network graphs can be both directed or undirected. In directed graphs, an edge (or arc) $e = (x, y)$ represents the social relationship from $x$ to $y$; note that this is not necessarily equal to the one from $y$ to $x$. On the other hand, in undirected graphs edges are assumed to be bidirectional, and therefore the properties of a social relationship between two nodes $x$ and $y$ is equal to the one from $y$ to $x$.

A network of connected nodes or individuals can be described using a number of simple indices. One of the most commonly used in social network

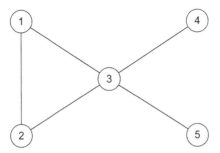

*Figure 2.1 Example of triplets and triangles.*

analysis is the *degree* of a node, which is a measure of the node's centrality. Centrality indicates the importance of a node and its influence over other nodes in the network. Degree centrality is defined as the number of edges connected to a node. It is important because the degree tells us the number of social relationships a node has, and therefore how many individuals in a social network are socially connected. In the case of directed graphs, there is a distinction between the in-degree, that is the number of incoming edges of the node, and the out-degree, the number of its outgoing edges.

The *path length* is another typical index. It can be intuitively seen as the distance between pairs of nodes in the network. This is important for understanding phenomena such as information diffusion, since the path length is directly related to the degree of connectivity of the graph (i.e. the property of nodes to be connected to each other in a unique graph component, without forming separate sub-graphs). A path between two nodes $x$ and $y$ in a graph is defined as a series of edges connecting a sequence of distinct nodes, where $x$ is the first node of the sequence and $y$ is the last one. Note that there could exist multiple paths between the same nodes. The length of a path is measured as the number of edges it contains. The shortest path between two nodes is the path with the shortest length. The *diameter* of a network is the length of the longest 'shortest path' between any pair of nodes in the network.

Two additional centrality indices can be defined using paths. The first is the *closeness* of a node. It is calculated as the inverse of the sum of the length of the shortest paths between the node and all the other nodes in the network. Nodes with high closeness are closer to all the other nodes than is the average node. For this reason, they have more influence and a more central role. Another measure of centrality based on paths is the *betweenness* of a node $v$, $g(v)$, defined as:

$$g(v) = \sum_{s \neq v \neq t} \frac{\sigma_{st}(v)}{\sigma_{st}} \qquad (2.1)$$

where $\sigma_{st}$ is the number of shortest paths from $s$ to $t$ and $\sigma_{st}(v)$ is the number of those paths in which one of the nodes is $v$. The node betweenness is particularly important in the analysis of information diffusion, for example, for identifying influential nodes or opinion leaders. In fact, since nodes with high betweenness are placed on a large number of paths, they are often fundamental to the spread of information, and act as opinion leaders.

Another important index in complex network analysis is the degree of *clustering*, which indicates how much nodes are interconnected to each other. Intuitively, a maximally clustered network is a full mesh, where all nodes are directly connected to all the other nodes. There are two clustering indices: the global and the local clustering coefficients. The global clustering coefficient of a network, $C$, is defined as follows:

$$C = \frac{3 \times \text{Number of triangles}}{\text{Number of connected triplets}} \qquad (2.2)$$

where a triplet of vertices consists of three connected vertices. For example, nodes 1, 3 and 5 in Figure 2.1 form a triplet. On the other hand, a triangle is composed of three vertices connected to each other by three edges, as nodes 1, 2 and 3 in Figure 2.1. $C$ is also referred to as transitivity.

The local clustering coefficient of a node $i$, $C_i$, measures how much $i$ and its neighbours are clustered, and it is defined as follows:

$$C_i = \frac{\text{Number of triangles centred at } i}{\text{Number of triplets centred at } i} \qquad (2.3)$$

The average of the local clustering coefficients of all nodes in the network, defined as $\overline{C} = \frac{1}{n} \sum_{i=1}^{n} C_i$, where $n$ is the number of nodes in the network, is an alternative to the global clustering coefficient. However, $\overline{C}$ is more influenced by nodes with low degree compared to $C$ [9].

Finally, we briefly highlight other indices often used in social network analysis. The correlation between the degrees of adjacent vertices, also called the *assortativity* [11], tells us whether the degree of the individual nodes is similar to the degrees of their neighbours. The presence of assortativity has an important impact on the circulation of information or the spread of diseases in social networks. The infection of a node with high degree will cause a very quick spread of the disease if the neighbours of the infected node also have high degree; as a result, the disease can reach a large proportion of nodes in the network just in a few steps. In such cases, quarantining hubs and their direct neighbours can prevent large-scale epidemics.

The number of *connected components* in the graph and the distribution of their size are also important indices for characterising social networks. Social networks are often formed of a giant component of connected nodes that includes most of the nodes of the network, and a small fraction of disconnected sub-networks or single nodes [12]. The presence of a giant component of connected nodes ensures reachability of the nodes through chains of social links and is often essential for the diffusion of information.

Another set of indices indicates the presence of *communities* in the network, that is, subsets of nodes with many connections to each other and fewer connections to other subsets of nodes. Communities represent an internal organisation and subdivision of the network. Many different definitions of community have been formulated over the years and different indices have been defined to identify them. However, recent experiments on large-scale graphs evinced that not all the proposed community detection algorithms show a good performance, and only few of them lead to accurate results [13]. For a complete description of these methods we refer the reader to [14].

## 2.2.2 Key Results From Social Network Analysis

The tools derived from complex network analysis have allowed researchers to discover some characteristic topological properties that have been observed in a variety of social networks, and which are considered to be distinctive features of social networks.

Stanley Milgram pioneered social network analysis by empirically measuring the average shortest path length between people in the USA through his famous 'small-world' experiment. Milgram asked a random set of participants living in Nebraska to send a package to a person in Boston, MA, by forwarding it only to people they directly knew, and whom they thought might be closer to the final recipient than they were. Each time an intermediate peer received the package, she had to add her name on it before sending it on, so that the number of intermediate steps could be traced. Some packages got lost, but those that reached the final destination had been through an average number of just six steps [15].

Milgram's findings were the first indication that social networks show an average shortest path length of around six. This fact is often identified as the 'six degrees of separation', and has been ascribed iconic status as a theoretical 'fact'. Short paths are a typical feature of many complex networks. In general, a network is said to have short paths if the average shortest path length is proportional to the logarithm of the number of nodes in the network, see Equation 2.6. A small average shortest path length in a social network is a favourable condition for the diffusion of information since it implies that messages travelling through chains of social links can reach any node in a few hops.

An average shortest path length of around six has been found in several studies of large-scale social networks. One of the most noticeable of these is represented by the work reported in [16], where the authors found that the social network representing contacts in Microsoft Messenger exhibits an average shortest path length of 6.6. A recent analysis of the entire Facebook social network graph, as of 2011, revealed an average shortest path length of 4.7 [17]. Similar results have also been found in analysis of Twitter social networks based on *following* relationships between users [18, 19]. Twitter shows a slightly smaller average shortest path length compared to Facebook, perhaps due to the peculiar nature of *following* relationships, which probably represent a weaker social relationship between users than is the case for Facebook friendships. Interestingly, Google+ shows an average shortest path length around 5 [20], appearing to be similar to Facebook and Twitter. These results seem to indicate that in online social networks (OSNs) the average distance between people can be even shorter than in offline environments, and consequently information could travel faster through social media compared to more traditional communication channels. Notice that these analyses only consider unweighted social graphs, where an edge indicates only the mere existence of a social contact between users. For this reason, the average shortest path length could be influenced by the presence of many inactive social relationships or ones with a very low frequency of interaction. For some types of information, these links might not be used, resulting in effective path lengths longer than those social network analysis would predict. We consider this point in more detail in Section 2.3.

Thanks to the work done by Duncan Watts and Steven Strogatz, social network graphs have been further characterised. In fact, compared to other kinds of networks such as biological and technological networks, social networks show not only a small average shortest path length but also high clustering [21]. In Section 2.2.3, the difference between high and low values of clustering will be discussed in more detail, with a comparison between random graphs and other types of structured networks. Here we recall that, with the presence of high clustering, there is a high probability that two neighbours connected to a node will also be connected to each other. A high clustering coefficient has been found in Microsoft Messenger [16], Facebook [17], Twitter [18], Google+ [20] and many other social networks [22]. Networks showing both a small average shortest path length and high clustering are called *small-world networks*. Notably, many social networks (including Facebook and Twitter [17, 18]) appear to be small-world networks.

Albert-László Barabási and Réka Albert observed that various social networks show node degree distributions that have a power law form [23]. A power law function has the following form:

$$f(x) = Cx^{-\alpha} \tag{2.4}$$

where $\alpha$ is called the scaling exponent, and 'scaling' means that a power law function satisfies $f(cx) \propto f(x)$. That is to say, the function's argument changes the constant of proportionality, but the shape of the function itself remains the same. This property is called scale invariance, and it leads to a linear relationship between the logarithm of both $f(x)$ and $x$. A power law function plotted on logarithmic scale for both axes appears as a straight line. The value of $\alpha$ controls the shape of the function, and thus the slope of the straight line on a logarithmic scale.

A quantity $x$ obeys a power law if it is drawn from a probability distribution $p(x)$ with the following form:

$$p(x) \propto x^{-\alpha} \tag{2.5}$$

Typically, estimated values of $\alpha$ derived from empirical data sets with quantities following power laws lie between 2 and 3 [24]. These values are typical also for node degree distributions in social networks. In power law node degree distributions, the higher the values of $\alpha$, the lower the probability of having nodes with high degree.

Networks with power law degree distributions are called *scale-free networks*. In these networks, most of the nodes have a very small degree, but there are a few nodes (called hubs) with many connections. The study of a large-scale phone call social network revealed a power law node degree distribution, with the presence of small local clusters typically grouped around a high-degree node [25]. Power law degree distributions have also been found in social networks formed of contacts extracted from email exchanges [26] and in OSNs like Facebook [27] (although this has been later contradicted in [17]) and Twitter [18], among others [22]. Scale-free networks have a higher robustness to fault tolerance compared to other kinds of networks, as observed in [16]. In fact, the failure (or removal) of random edges does not drastically modify the structure of the network in such cases. To deeply modify the graph, hubs need to be identified and removed, and the probability of selecting their edges from a random selection is lower than the probability of selecting edges from low degree nodes, since the latter are more common than the former [28]. Scale-free networks could, nonetheless, suffer from targeted attacks on hubs.

Social networks also show positive assortativity, as found in the Facebook social graph [17, 27], Twitter [19] and other OSNs, including Flickr, YouTube, LiveJournal and Orkut [22]. Nodes in social networks are, on average, linked to similar others, not only in terms of node degree, as already seen for the assortativity. This general property is known as homophily [29], and is known to directly influence many aspects of social networks. Homophily is known to be the result of two underlying mechanisms: *selection* and *social influence*, where the former indicates the propensity of people to create new social relationships with people who are similar to them, and the latter indicates that people influence the behaviour of their friends and, as a result, socially connected people tend to become similar to each other. In their seminal work, Christakis and Fowler [30] analysed the interplay of these effects in a social network with information about health-related outcomes. They found that obese and non-obese people tended to clusert in the network, in accordance with homophily. In addition, they found that selection alone is not enough to explain this clusterisation, which is, in part, the result of social influence. This means that obesity (and perhaps other behavioural-related health conditions) may be related to some kind of intrinsic spreading effect of social networks [31].

The analysis of many different social networks (e.g. the studies on Facebook [32] and Microsoft Messenger [16]) highlighted the presence of homophily in different characteristics of the users. Moreover, the presence of a giant component is clearly visible in the social graphs of Facebook [17], Twitter [19], mobile phone networks [25] and Microsoft Messenger [16]. Another property of the topology of social networks is the presence of spatial constraints. Nodes in the same cluster are more likely to be spatially close to each other, whereas nodes in different clusters are usually in different geographical regions [33]. Also the mobility of nodes has been found to play a central role in the formation of social relationships, since nodes encountering each other can exchange information and form or strengthen social relationships [34].

In Table 2.1, we report the properties of several OSNs (e.g. Facebook and Twitter). For comparison purposes, we also report some reference results from the analysis of offline social networks, as well as key results related to the network structures of the Internet itself, or Internet systems such as World Wide Web (WWW). This allows us to summarise the key properties highlighted in the literature about the structure of OSN unweighted graphs, and to compare them with other types of networks analysed using a similar approach. In the literature, initial results on node degree of social networks seemed to indicate that power law distributions are a distinctive feature of social and technological networks. However, several analyses found results that contradict this conventional assumption (e.g. the work by Ugander et al. [17] on the Facebook social graph). In accordance with what we have already discussed in this chapter, the average shortest path length of OSNs appears to be shorter than that found in other kinds of networks, for example, the WWW and some co-authorship networks. Note that the co-authorship network from biology shows a very short average shortest path length compared to typical values for offline social networks. This could be due to the number of coauthors per paper, since this is usually much higher in biology than in other disciplines (see http://www.harzing.com/data_metrics_comparison.htm), and it is higher than the typical group size in humans. The difference in terms of average shortest path length between OSNs and other kinds of social networks, however, seems to be true only when we consider the unweighted social graph of OSNs. When interaction graphs are considered instead, the average shortest path length is in line with the results found offline and with the theory of six degrees of separation. Nevertheless, only a few analyses have been performed to highlight this difference (e.g. the work by Wilson et al. [27]), and more work is needed to verify it. Although the values of clustering coefficient for the different networks can vary significantly, all of them denote high clusterisation in the network. Since OSNs show high clustering and short paths they can

# Table 2.1 Structural Properties of Several Social Networks

| Network[a] | Vertices | Edges | Degree Distribution[b] | Avg. Shortest Path | Diameter | Local Clustering | Global Clust. | Giant Comp. Size (%) | Assortativity |
|---|---|---|---|---|---|---|---|---|---|
| Facebook [17] | 721M | 68.7G | Long-tailed with cutoff | 4.7 | – | – | – | 99.91 | 0.226 |
| Facebook[c] [27] Social | 10.7M | 240M | Long-tailed | 4.8 | 13.4 | 0.164 | – | – | 0.17 |
| Interaction | – | | PL $1.5 < \alpha < 1.8$ | $5 < l < 10$ | $18 < d < 25$ | $0.03 < \overline{C} < 0.08$ | – | – | $0.18 < \rho < 0.23$ |
| Twitter [19] | 41.7M | 1.47G | PL $\alpha = 2.276$ | 4.12 | 18 | – | – | – | – |
| Twitter [18] | 175M | 20G | PL $\alpha = 1.35$ (i) PL $\alpha = 1.28$ (o) LN $\mu = 2.8, \sigma^2 = 3.4$ (i) LN $\mu = 3.6, \sigma^2 = 2.9$ (o) | 4.17 (u) 4.05 (d) | 18 | | | 92.9 | −0.296 (i) 0.272 (o) |
| Google+ [20] | 35.1M | 575M | PL $\alpha = 1.35$ (i) PL $\alpha = 1.2$ (o) | 5.9 (d) 4.7 (u) | 19 (d) 13 (u) | – | – | 71.8 | – |
| Messenger [16] | 180M | 1.34G | PL $\alpha = 0.8$ | 6.6 | 29 | 0.137 | – | 99.9 | – |
| Flickr [22] | 1.85M | 22.6M | PL $\alpha = 1.78$ (i) PL $\alpha = 1.74$ (o) | 5.67 | 27 | – | – | – | 0.202 |
| Yahoo 360! [35] | 5M | 7M | PL shape | 8.26 | – | – | – | – | – |
| Myspace [36] | 100K | 6.85M | PL $\alpha = 3.1$ | 2.7 | – | 0.26 | – | – | 0.02 |
| Orkut [22] | 3.07M | 224M | PL $\alpha = 1.5$ (i) PL $\alpha = 1.5$ (o) | 4.25 | 9 | – | – | – | 0.072 |
| LiveJournal [22] | 5.28M | 77.4M | PL $\alpha = 1.65$ (i) PL $\alpha = 1.59$ (o) | 5.88 | 20 | – | – | – | 0.179 |

| | | | | | | | | | |
|---|---|---|---|---|---|---|---|---|---|
| Youtube [22] | 1.16M | 4.95M | PL $\alpha$ = 1.99 (i)<br>PL $\alpha$ = 1.63 (o) | 5.1 | 21 | – | – | – | –0.033 |
| Cyworld [36] | 12M | 191M | PL $\alpha \sim$ 2 (first region)<br>$\alpha \sim$ 5 (second region) | 3.2 | – | 0.16 | – | – | –0.13 |
| Sina Weibo [37] | 80.8M | 7.2G | PL $\alpha$ = 2.33 (i) | 4.63 | 14 | – | – | 76.8 | 0.15 |
| Renren [38] | 42.1M | 1.66G | PL $\alpha$ = 3.5 (limited region) | 5.38 | – | 0.063 | – | – | – |
| Co-authorship [39] | | | | | | | | | |
| Biology | 1.52M | – | – | 4.6 | 24 | – | 0.066 | 92 | 0.13 |
| Physics | 52.9K | – | – | 5.9 | 20 | – | 0.43 | 85 | 0.36 |
| Mathematics | 253K | – | – | 7.6 | 27 | – | 0.15 | 82 | 0.12 |
| Email [40] | 16.9K | 57K | Long-tailed | – | – | – | 0.168 | – | – |
| Phone calls [25] | 4.6M | 7M | PL $\alpha$ = 8.4 | – | – | – | – | – | – |
| WWW [41] | 203M | 1.47G | PL $\alpha$ = 2.1 (i)<br>PL $\alpha$ = 2.72 (o) | 6.83 | 28 | – | – | 91 | – |
| Internet [42] | 3.89K | 5.01K | PL $\alpha$ = 0.48 | – | – | – | – | – | – |

[a] Letters in parentheses indicate whether the graph is directed (d) or undirected (u) and whether the in-degree (i) or the out-degree (o) is analysed.

[b] Fitted parameters for power law (PL) or log-normal (LN) distributions, or indication on the shape of the distribution.

[c] Average values out of several Facebook regional networks. The number of vertices and edges are the total sum for all the regional networks.

be considered small-world networks, as highlighted by several studies in the literature. Interestingly, the size of the giant component ranges between ~70% and more than 99.9%, denoting a significant difference amongst networks in their ability to interconnect nodes with each other, and form a unique connected component. Notably, this variation can be noted in all types of networks, indicating that it is not characteristic of a specific environment. As far as assortativity is concerned, most of the networks are weakly assortative (i.e. with positive assortativity), with a few exceptions showing the opposite. This means that nodes tend, with a weakly marked preference, to establish social relationships with nodes with similar degree.

From these results, we can note that OSNs show structural properties similar to other types of social and technological networks. This indicates that, at the microscopic level, OSNs and offline social networks seem to have the same structure.

### 2.2.3 Models for the Generation of Network Graphs

Besides observing social networks though complex network indices, many studies have proposed mathematical models to generate graphs that present the key features observed in real networks.

After observing the properties of small-world networks, Watts and Strogatz (WS) introduced a generative model of small-world network graphs, known as the WS model. This model starts from a regular ring lattice graph, such as the one shown in Figure 2.2(a), where all the nodes have the same degree and, when placed on a ring, are connected only to their

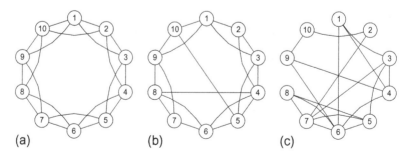

*Figure 2.2 Network graphs generated by the Watts–Strogats model with different parameters. (a) The network is a regular lattice and no modifications have been applied. (b) Some links have been modified so as to obtain a small-world network. (c) The modification of a high percentage of links leads to a random graph.*

four closest neighbours on the ring. These kinds of regular graphs have a high clustering coefficient, but also a high shortest path length, which makes them unsuitable for modelling social networks. The algorithm of the WS model allows us to rewire these regular graphs by introducing some short-cut edges, thus connecting distant regions of the ring, as shown in Figure 2.2(b). These short-cuts allow high clustering, but also permit a small average shortest path length (i.e. a path length that increases as the logarithm of the number of nodes). The resulting graph is a small-world network. In effect, the WS model adds a certain degree of randomness to a regular graph. If in a small-world network the level of randomness is further increased, the result is a purely random graph, as the one shown in Figure 2.2(c). A random graph can also be generated by the fundamental Erdős–Rényi model, where each possible pair of links in the graph has a probability $p$ of generating an edge to each of the other nodes [43]. The clustering coefficient of a random graph is proportional to $1/N$, where $N$ is the number of nodes. A network is considered to be very clustered if its clustering coefficient is higher than that of a random graph with the same number of nodes and with the same average degree. Small-world networks have higher clustering than their corresponding random graphs [21]. In addition, in small-world networks, the average shortest path length, $L$, grows as the logarithm of the number of nodes:

$$L \propto \log N \tag{2.6}$$

The degree distribution of a network graph generated with the WS model is relatively homogeneous, whilst many real social networks show degree distributions that are asymptotically power law, as already discussed in Section 2.2.2. In addition, another limitation to the WS model is the fact that it does not consider network growth. It implies a fixed number of nodes and does not allow the network to grow over time. This means that the WS model cannot be used to analyse network dynamics and its evolution.

Several generative models of scale-free networks are present in the literature. The most famous is probably the Barabási–Albert model (or simply BA model), named after its inventors Albert–László Barabási and Réka Albert [23]. This model is based on the preferential attachment mechanism (also known as 'rich get richer'), for which the higher the degree of a node the higher the probability that new nodes will create social links with it. This process naturally supports network growth. Nodes are added to the graph one at a time, following the preferential attachment rule. The

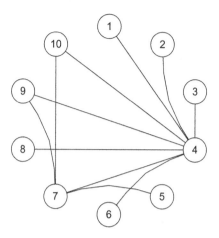

Figure 2.3 A scale-free network obtained from the BA model. Node 4 is a hub with many connections, whereas most of the other nodes have only few links.

result is a scale-free network graph. A small scale-free network with 10 nodes obtained from the BA model is shown in Figure 2.3. The presence of a hub is clearly visible in the figure. Graphs generated with the BA model have been shown to have node degree distributions compliant with those of many different real network graphs, such as the WWW [23]. Moreover, the BA model produces graphs with average shortest path length $L$ that grows logarithmically with the number of nodes in the network ($N$), with the addition of a double logarithmic correction:

$$L \propto \frac{\log N}{\log \log N} \tag{2.7}$$

However, the BA model does not produce high clustering, and therefore it is not necessarily the best model for social network analysis.

## 2.3 FROM SOCIAL GRAPHS TO INTERACTION GRAPHS

The analyses of social networks described so far, both in offline and online environments, only consider unweighted ties. This means that links in social network graphs represent the mere existence of a social relationship between the individuals concerned, and all relationships are considered to have the same level of importance. This is often not representative enough of real social relationships. From sociology, it is known that the importance of social relationships is highly inhomogeneous and relationships assume different roles at different levels of strength. Recently, in [27], Wilson and colleagues demonstrated that there is a significant difference between the properties of a large-scale sub-network of the Facebook graph with or without considering the interaction level between users. Graphs where links are weighted by the interaction level between the users they connect are usually called interaction graphs. In [44], the unweighted social graph extracted from publicly available data on Google+ was augmented with node attributes and interaction data between users. The results confirm that the properties of interaction graphs are significantly different from the properties of the equivalent unweighted network. Another study revealed that the interaction graph from Facebook has a higher clustering coefficient, a lower average degree and higher average shortest path length and diameter than the equivalent unweighted graph [27]. In particular, the average shortest path length for Facebook is below 5 when the unweighted graph is considered [17], but is about 6 in the interaction graph. This is due to the presence of a high number of inactive social contacts for each user, and these represent short-cuts in the unweighted networks. Eliminating these contacts is fundamental for information diffusion analyses, for example, since the quantity of information (or infections) passing through inactive social relationships will obviously be zero.

The first serious attempt to consider the different roles of social relationships at different strength levels was conducted by the American sociologist Mark Granovetter. He argued that tie strength (i.e. the importance of a social tie), informally defined, in [45], as "*a (probably linear) combination of time, emotional intensity, intimacy and the reciprocal services which characterise the tie,*" determines the functional properties of a social relationship. Social ties can be broadly divided in two categories: *strong* and *weak* ties. The former are related to a small set of intimate friends and are useful for consolidating a core group of trusted people. On the other hand, weak ties consist of acquaintances, socially far from the ego and usually included within different social milieux (i.e. tied to individuals not tied to ego) [45]. Granovetter found that, despite their low strength, weak ties are important to individuals for accessing resources from other social groups, and their total strength exceeds that of strong ties since they are large in number. Granovetter's findings remind us that tie strength must be taken into account to understand fully social aspects of a social network.

Tie strength determines important local structural elements in social networks. First of all, let us focus on triads, that is, triplets of nodes connected to each other. In social networks, two individuals with strong social relation-ships with a common third individual are likely to have a social relationship with each other (either strong or weak). This property is called triadic clo-sure [45]. It has been recently shown that triadic closure has a direct impact on the formation of power law degree distributions in social networks [46]. Moreover, the high clustering coefficient in social networks is intuitively influenced by the presence of triadic closure. As a consequence of triadic closure, local bridges, that is, links connecting nodes with no neighbours in common, are generally weak ties. To better understand why, consider the example in Figure 2.4. In the figure, strong ties are bold lines, whereas weak ties are thin lines. If we take a local bridge, for example the link connecting nodes 5 and 6, the nodes it connects cannot have common neighbours by definition. If link 5–6 was a strong tie, for triadic closure to hold, there would have to be, with high probability, links connecting 5 with the strong-tie neighbours of 6, that is, 3 and 4, and, similarly, there would have to be, with high probability, links between 6 and the strong-tie neighbours of 5, that is, 1 and 2. However, the presence of these links would violate the definition of a local bridge, for which the connected nodes must not have common neighbours. Note that links connecting regions of the network otherwise completely disconnected from each other are simply called bridges (as opposed to local bridges), and are much rarer than local bridges in social net-works. Nevertheless, bridges are of strategic importance for the circulation

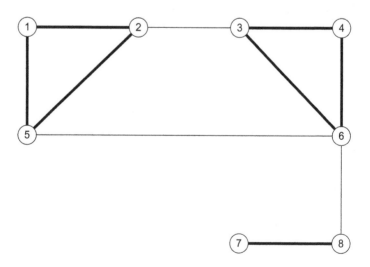

*Figure 2.4 An example of network graph containing two local bridges and a bridge.*

of information, since they connect otherwise separated parts of the network. In Figure 2.4, the link connecting 6 and 8 is an example of abridge.

When three nodes form a triad (i.e. are connected to each other) with three strong ties (thus forming a clique), these ties are called simmelian ties [47]. Simmelian ties are considered to be the building blocks of social networks, as pairs of individuals involved in a simmelian tie are more likely to cooperate with each other, and simmelian ties are usually more stable over time than non-simmelian ties [48]. The change from dyad to triad or larger groups changes individuals' behaviour drastically, and when people are involved in groups their behaviour is more predictable [49]. As a consequence, individuals with more simmelian ties tend to be less individualistic, with reduced bargaining power, and enhanced conflict resolution [47]. When an individual is involved in multiple simmelian ties, she is part of different cliques and she will face different sets of role expectations. The more a person is able to broker simmelian ties, the more productive she appears to be.

A problem with analyses involving tie strength is that the latter is generally not directly measurable since it is composed of some emotional factors that are not really identifiable in the kinds of variables used to create networks. Nevertheless, Peter Marsden demonstrated the feasibility of constructing measures of tie strength through multiple indicator techniques [50]. Marsden built an analytical model to explain the relation between tie strength and a set of social indicators (emotional closeness, duration, frequency of contact, breadth of discussion topics and confiding). The results of his analysis demonstrated that emotional closeness (or emotional intensity) is the best indicator of the strength of a social relationship. Moreover, measures of the time spent in a relationship (e.g. frequency of contact and duration) are also related to tie strength, even though they tend to systematically overestimate tie strength when the involved persons are co-workers or neighbours. These results indicate that tie strength can be effectively estimated using empirically measurable indicators. As will be clear in the following chapters, this fact has made it possible to undertake a series of analyses on the interaction graph of social networks from observable traces of communication data, easily accessible from offline and online communication systems.

Finally, tie strength is the key element determining the structure of ego networks. Clearly, if tie strength is not considered, any ego network is just a star structure centred on the ego, and does not present any particularly interesting properties.

## 2.4 MICROSCOPIC PROPERTIES OF SOCIAL NETWORKS

Microscopic-level analyses typically take into account only the set of personal social relationships of individual users, which are usually known as ego networks.

More formally, an ego network is the social network formed of an individual (called ego) and all the persons with whom the ego has a social link (referred to as the alters). Ego networks are useful to study the properties of human social behaviour at a personal level, and to assess the extent to which individual characteristics of the ego affect the size and the composition of their network. One of the most important results found on ego networks is that the cognitive constraints of the human brain and the limited time that a person can use for socialising directly impact on the structural properties of ego networks. This result is derivative of what has become known as the *social brain hypothesis* (SBH). The SBH explains the extraordinary evolution of human brain not in terms of making and using tools, but, instead, in terms of the need to maintain an increasing number of social relationships to survive against challenging environmental conditions [51].

Maintaining social relationships is demanding in terms of cognitive resources, because one needs both memory capacity to remember and manage facts about social peers, and time capacity to interact with them. Therefore, the SBH predicts that, as the size of the brain increased during the primate evolution, so also has the typical size of social groups [52].

Evidence to confirm the SBH has come from a series of studies on primates that demonstrate a positive correlation between the size of a species' neocortex and the size of its social groups [51]. Indeed, neuroimaging studies have since shown that this relationship also holds within species between individuals: in both humans [53–56] and macaques [57], individuals who have more friends have more brain tissue in certain key areas of the brain, notably in the frontal lobes.

Whilst for most primates it is relatively easy to identify their social group size from direct observation, this is difficult for humans, due to the structural complexity of human societies in which large ego networks are completely interconnected with each other, and thus difficult to isolate. Extrapolating from the data collected on primates, the number of social relationships that humans can actively maintain over time (i.e. by investing a non-negligible amount of cognitive and time resources) has been predicted to be, on average, around 150. This number is known as *Dunbar's number*, and its existence has been confirmed by several analyses on data extracted from censuses or collected from questionnaires [58, 59].

Recently, analyses of Twitter data have demonstrated that the average intensity of communication of each user towards all her friends (as a function of the number of social contacts of the user) is asymptotic, and this is ascribable to the limits imposed by Dunbar's number [60]. This evidence for the existence of a Dunbar's number in OSNs has paved the way for further and more detailed analyses on the structure of ego networks in OSNs that will be presented in later chapters. To better understand these results, it will be helpful first to describe the basic properties of ego social networks in a little more detail.

### 2.4.1 Layered Structure of Ego Networks

Inside their social groups, humans form small coalitions with other individuals to provide mutual support and to reduce the frequency of aggression or harassment [61], thereby reducing some of the costs of group living. This strategy is used at different levels, from small groups of one or two strong allies, to larger groups of people sharing the same interests or goals. The fact that, inside a social group, the ego interacts with alters at different levels of intensity is the key reason behind the structural properties found in human ego networks. Specifically, ego networks show a typical hierarchical structure of a series of sub-groupings arranged in a hierarchical inclusive sequence, that in human ego networks is typically formed of four or five layers. An individual ego can be envisaged as sitting at the centre of a series of concentric circles of alters ordered by the strength of their social ties [62], as shown in Figure 2.5. Each of these circles has a characteristic size and frequency of contact between the ego and the alters contained in it. These circles are hierarchically inclusive in that each circle includes everyone in the circles within it, plus additional alters specific to that circle. The first circle, called the *support clique*, contains alters with very strong social relationships with the ego, informally identified in literature as *intimate* or *best friends*. These alters are people contacted by the ego in circumstances of strong emotional distress or financial disaster. These are the people one can rely on to help out when all else fails. The size of this circle is limited, on average, to 5 members, usually contacted by the ego at least once a week. The second circle, known as the *sympathy group*, also contains alters who can be identified as *close friends*. This circle contains on average 15

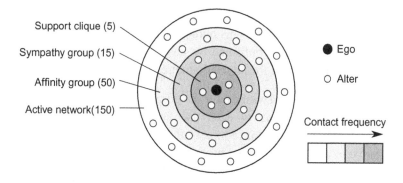

Figure 2.5 *The ego network model.*

members who are contacted by the ego at least once a month. The next circle is the *affinity group* (or *band* in the ethnographic literature), which contains 50 alters, usually including also more casual friends or extended family members [63]. The last circle in the ego network model is the *active network*, which, including all the other circles, totals about 150 members, and is typically dominated by extended family members and more distant friends. This circle is bounded by the limit of Dunbar's number and contains people for whom the ego actively invests a non-negligible amount of resources in order to maintain relationships over time. People in the active network are contacted at least once a year. Alters beyond the active network are considered inactive, since they are not contacted regularly by the ego. These alters are grouped in additional external circles, which in the ethnographic literature are referred to as *mega-bands* and *tribes*, but which we might think of as constituting acquaintances and people whose faces we recognise. They extend to layers of ~500 and ~1500 individuals, respectively. For a complete discussion about the properties of these circles we refer the reader to [61].

An interesting property of the circular structure of ego networks is that circles have a scaling ratio of about 3 – in other words, each circle is three times larger than the one immediately inside it. This layered structure with scaling ratio of 3 has been identified within both egocentric social networks and the organisation of hunter-gatherer societies [58, 64, 65], as well as in the social systems of the more socially complex mammal species such as elephants, killer whales and anthropoid primates [66]. More importantly, perhaps, within the hierarchical structure of an ego network we find an additional important sociological structuring, namely the division between family (kin), friends and acquaintances. Whilst acquaintances appear only in the layer between 150 and 500, family and friends are more or less equally divided within each of the layers out to the 150 layer – albeit with a tendency for the 50 layer to contain more friends and the outermost 150 layer to contain more family (mainly extended family) [67]. In part, this is due to the fact that the support given by kin to the ego is less conditional on contact frequency than is the case for the support given by friends, a phenomenon known as the 'kinship premium' [63, 67]. In fact, a distant kin with low contact frequency with ego will typically provide much more support than a friend at the same level of contact frequency.

Extrapolating backwards from the pattern of the circles shown in Figure 2.5 suggests that there might be an additional innermost circle formed of just one or two alters – or, to be more precise, this layer should average about 1.5 alters. The presence of this layer, containing very strong relationships, such as a partner or a particularly intimate friend, has not yet been identified in offline social networks, perhaps because the available communication data lack sufficient precision to show it. However, as we show in the next chapter, evidence for the existence of this innermost layer has come from data provided by OSNs, thanks mainly to the quantity and the quality of the communication data obtainable from online social platforms.

## 2.4.2 Extended Ego Networks and Structural Holes

The definition of ego network given in Section 2.4.1 is based only on direct social relationships between the ego and her alters. This is the main definition used in anthropology and psychology. In fact, this linear description of a social network is just one way of describing an individual's social world. If we include the interactions between the alters (which we refer to as mutual friendship relationships), we have a more conventional network, which will often consist of sets of semi-disconnected sub-networks (connected by the ego) representing different groups of friends and family. We call these networks *extended ego networks*. They are useful for studying the local topology of social networks around single individuals, and, for example, for the analysis of the formation of triads and simmelian ties, as well as functional sub-networks (usually in the outer two layers) that represent sets of friends from different parts of ego's social life (e.g. family members, former friends from school or college, hobby club friends, church friends, work friends, etc.) that often do not overlap. In addition to the local clustering coefficient that we encountered in Section 2.2.1, additional measures of clustering can be calculated on extended ego networks. One of these is *network constraint*. As in the case of local clustering, this metric quantifies the extent to which the alters connected to the ego are also connected to each other. An extended ego network containing social contacts with low tie strength and without common connections has a low network constraint. On the other hand, the presence of many alters with strong ties that are also strongly interconnected to each other is associated with a high network constraint. When network constraint is low, the ego appears to be the only bridge connecting otherwise well-separated portions of her extended ego network. Since these parts would be disconnected without the presence of the ego, they are called *structural holes*. The more structural holes in an extended ego network, the higher the importance of the role of the ego in the maintenance of a link between the different social subgroups [68]. The ego can also benefit from the presence of structural holes for access to information coming from different social groups and thus different sources. On the other hand, a highly clustered or highly constrained extended ego network is not favourable for the circulation of information since information could remain trapped in cliques and not be passed on to other subgroups [45]. One implication is that individuals with extended ego networks with more structural holes usually have a higher social status compared to others. Ron Burt proposed an index to measure the level of constraint in an extended ego network starting from a measure of constraint $c_{ij}$ between two nodes $i$ and $j$:

$$c_{ij} = \left( p_{ij} + \sum_q p_{iq} \times p_{qj} \right)^2 , \quad i \neq q \neq j \tag{2.8}$$

where $p_{ij}$ is the percentage of tie strength between $i$ and $j$ with respect to the total sum of the tie strength of all the social links of $i$. Tie strength can be binary in case of unweighted graphs. $c_{ij}$ measures the sum of the direct and indirect portion of tie strength between $i$ and $j$. A value close to 1 denotes the presence of a very strong relationship or a relationship in a highly clustered region, and it is associated with a high constraint. If all the relationships of the ego have a high constraint, then the extended ego network is also highly constrained. The constraint index of an ego $i$, $C_i$, is defined as the sum of the constraint on its individual dyadic relationships:

$$C_i = \sum_j c_{ij}, \quad i \neq j \tag{2.9}$$

A recent analysis on Twitter found that extended ego networks with more structural holes are associated with opinion leaders whose tweets often cover a diverse range of topics [69]. Through a classification of tweets in two emotional categories (happy and sad), these authors also found that people expressing similar emotions in their tweets tend to cluster together – another example of the phenomenon of homophily that we met earlier.

Although these results give a first insight into the constrained nature of OSNs, revealing a similarity between online and offline human social behaviour, there is still a great lack of knowledge about all the other ego network structural properties of OSNs. Specifically, it is not clear whether structures similar to those described by the ego network model and found offline are also present in OSNs.

## 2.5 BRIDGING MICROSCOPIC AND MACROSCOPIC PROPERTIES OF SOCIAL NETWORKS

Analyses combining both macroscopic and microscopic properties of social networks are called meso-level analyses. These kinds of studies are aimed at better understanding how the properties of ego networks and of social aspects of individuals' behaviour impact on the formation of the high-level structures observed in complete social network graphs, and vice versa. Clearly, these kinds of analyses require multidisciplinary approaches to the study of social networks since they span from the behaviour and the psychological properties of the human brain to mathematical models for the description of social network graphs. Even though a convergence between macroscopic and microscopic analyses is essential for achieving a full understanding of social networks, the results obtained so far by meso-level analyses are still very preliminary.

An example of a meso-level analysis is the work presented in [70], where the authors propose a new generative model of social network graphs able to create a synthetic weighted network with a set of microscopic and macroscopic properties given as input that is compatible with the results in the literature. Specifically, the model takes as input the size of the network to be generated, the distribution of the size of the ego networks and of the size of the different ego network layers, the distribution of the tie strengths within each layer, and a parameter $p$ that indicates the probability of triadic closure (i.e. closing triplets to form triangles) in the creation of local bridges. The model also considers spatial constraints, giving a higher probability to the formation of strong ties between nodes that are in proximity than between nodes that are far from each other. The model has a bottom-up approach, starting from the generation of ego networks maintaining the structural properties seen in Section 2.4.1 and the properties given as input.

Whilst they are being generated, ego networks are also combined together, forming a complete social network graph. To combine ego networks, each ego is associated with an agent, that, at discrete steps, adds a new alter into its ego network, placing it in one of its circles according to the defined distributions. Each agent stops when its network reaches the size that has been assigned to it. At each step, the agents that have not yet completed their ego network select a new node to connect to. This selection is made according to two strategies: triadic closure and bridging, picked with probability $p$ and $1 - p$, respectively.

For the triadic closure strategy, as shown in Figure 2.6, the agent $i$ selects a neighbour $k$ from the set of its neighbours, with a probability proportional to the tie strength and inversely proportional to the geographic distance from $k$. In this way, a physically close neighbour with high tie strength has a high probability of being selected. Hence, a neighbour $j$ of $k$ is chosen with the same principle applied to $k$. If all the neighbours of $k$ have already completed their ego networks, another node $k$ is selected, repeating the procedure until a suitable node $j$ is found. Then, $i$ adds $j$ to its ego network, and the tie strength of the new relationship is chosen according to the availability of space in the layers and the distribution of the tie strengths for each layer. If there are no nodes $j$ available, the bridging strategy is adopted. For the bridging strategy, $i$ chooses a node to add to its ego network

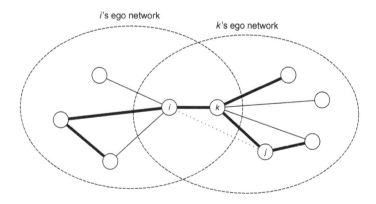

*Figure 2.6 Triadic closure strategy.*

with a probability proportional to the physical distance from the node and inversely proportional to the number of social contacts in common with it. This ensures the generation of local bridges in the network.

As reported in [70], this model is able to reproduce both macroscopic and microscopic properties of reference networks on which it has been validated. In particular, the model preserves the node's degree distribution, the average shortest path length and the clustering coefficient of the reference networks. In addition, validation of the model has been carried out on a large-scale interaction graph extracted from Facebook. The graph generated by the model also preserves the fundamental properties of the ego network model and the size and tie strength distribution of the layers compatible with those of the reference network.

Although this model provides a good fit to reality, there is still a lot of work to do to characterise fully some important aspects of social networks. Despite occasional claims to the contrary, these are in fact still poorly understood, especially in online environments. More importantly, perhaps, we have little understanding of how microscopic and macroscopic features are related to each other.

## 2.6 CHAPTER SUMMARY AND DISCUSSION

In this chapter, we presented the key reference literature on human social network analysis. This can be categorised according to whether the global properties of the networks are the main focus (*macroscopic* analysis), or whether the focus is on the local properties of users personal networks (*microscopic* analysis). We showed that, for the analysis of macroscopic properties, social networks can be represented as graphs. A first body of work looks at the network as an unweighted graph, which is typically called the *social* graph, and analyses it by means of complex network techniques. Then, we introduced the concept of tie strength that, by measuring the relative importance of social relationships between people, is a fundamental aspect to be considered. When tie strength is included in the description of social networks, the resulting graph is typically called an *interaction* graph, as the amount of interaction over a link is strongly correlated with tie strength. We also presented the microscopic properties of social networks, through the ego network model. The ego network model also considers tie strength, and is one of the reference models in the literature for the analysis of the microscopic properties of human social networks, and how they impact on properties observed at the macro scale. Finally, we presented a model for the generation of synthetic network graphs combining both microscopic and macroscopic properties of social networks.

The main 'take home messages' out of the work presented in the chapter are the following.

## Macroscopic Properties of Unweighted Social Networks

Social networks differ from other types of networks (e.g. biological and technological networks) in that they are both small-world, and sometimes, though not always, scale-free. Small-world networks show high clustering and small average shortest path length. On the other hand, scale-free networks exhibit a node degree distribution with power law form. The basic (and most important) models for the generation of synthetic network graphs are able to reproduce small-world or scale-free networks, but they typically fail to combine the two properties.

## From Social Graphs to Interaction Graphs

Considering tie strength is fundamental for the correct analysis of social networks. For example, when calculating the average shortest path length of a network, the resulting value could be significantly smaller in an unweighted graph than in the equivalent interaction graph. Nonetheless, in unweighted graphs (especially for OSNs), many social links have null or very low tie strength, and should not really be considered, because they are never activated. Tie strength is also directly connected to the formation of some important structural properties of social networks (e.g. the formation of local bridges as a consequence of triadic closure). Despite the importance of tie strength, relatively few analyses on OSN are focused on the interaction graph. Moreover, whilst tie strength has been characterised in detail in offline social networks, there have been few attempts to describe and estimate tie strength in online social interactions.

## Microscopic Properties of Social Networks

The main characteristics of offline ego networks are the presence of Dunbar's number, combined with their hierarchical structure defining a series of concentric circles of alters around the ego with typical properties in terms of emotional closeness, size and contact frequency. These properties are directly controlled by a combination of cognitive constraints imposed by the human brain and the limited amount of time that individuals have for socialising. Extended ego networks, in contrast to ego networks, consider not only the direct social relationships of the ego with her alters but also the relationships existing between these alters (i.e. mutual friendship relationships). The analysis of extended ego networks is important for identifying the formation of local topological structures around the ego such as structural holes.

**Bridging Microscopic and Macroscopic Properties of Social Networks**
The analysis of social networks can benefit from the combination of both macro- and micro-level analyses. We presented a model able to generate a social network graph that reproduces both local properties of ego networks, and global properties of entire network graphs. This is one of the few examples combining microscopic and macroscopic properties of social networks.

# CHAPTER 3

# Tie Strength and Ego Network Structure in Facebook

## 3.1 INTRODUCTION

In this chapter, we present the most recent advances in the area of the analysis of tie strength and ego networks in Facebook. In addition, we describe our contribution to the field, represented by two analyses: the first is aimed at modelling and predicting tie strength (Section 3.2), and the second is aimed at characterising the structural properties of ego networks in Facebook (Section 3.3). The key idea of our work is to create models to estimate tie strength through communication variables collected from Facebook, and then study the properties of ego networks defined by the estimated tie strengths. The results of our analyses give a detailed characterisation of the properties of the layered structure of ego networks in Facebook that was previously unknown.

For the prediction of tie strength, we study a small but very detailed dataset of Facebook communications. In order to describe in detail the nature of social interactions between the users in the dataset, we applied Principal Component Analysis (PCA) [71] to a set of variables that describe different aspects of the social relationships of the users. This allowed us to create models for the prediction of tie strength from the variables collected from Facebook.

Building on the results obtained on tie strength prediction, we analysed two large-scale Facebook datasets, using the contact frequency between users (the only information related to the relationships available from the datasets) to estimate tie strength. We studied the distribution of the contact frequency in each ego network extracted from the dataset to find out whether a layered structure similar to the one described by the offline ego network model could be found also in Facebook.

## 3.2 MODELLING TIE STRENGTH IN FACEBOOK

In this section, we discuss the possibility of estimating tie strength from Facebook data, and we show that the contact frequency in Facebook is a good predictor of tie strength. The results presented in this section provide a solid basis for the analysis of social relationships and ego networks in online environments.

To characterise the tie strength in Facebook, we carried out a detailed investigation on the factors underlying social interactions in the online environment. We introduce the background work in the field in Section 3.2.1, and we motivate the need for more detailed analyses on the nature of tie strength in online social networks (OSNs). Then, we present our contribution. We used detailed data about social relationships and interactions in Facebook of a controlled set of Facebook users through a Facebook application created for the purpose, as explained in Section 3.2.2. By using PCA, as described in Section 3.2.3, we show the presence of factors in Facebook interaction data that are qualitatively compatible with the tie strength dimensions by Granovetter's definition. This enables the possibility of modelling tie strength from Facebook interaction variables. Building on this result, in Section 3.2.4, we present a series of models for the prediction of tie strength, testing several possible combinations of predictors extracted from Facebook. We also assessed the accuracy of a model that uses the contact frequency between users as the sole predictor of tie strength, and we compare the goodness of fit of this model with that of more complete ones. The former is the typical model used in OSN analysis, and is the model we adopted for the analysis of ego networks in Facebook and Twitter datasets, which will be presented in Section 3.3 and in Chapters 4 and 5, respectively.

### 3.2.1 Background Work

The possibility of obtaining an accurate estimation of tie strength from Facebook data was initially noted by Gilbert and Karahalios [72]. The variables used to estimate tie strength, through a regression model, were chosen by these authors to cover all the tie strength dimensions hypothesised by Granovetter in his informal definition (i.e. time, emotional intensity, intimacy and reciprocal services which characterise tie relationship – see Section 2.3 for the complete definition). The results indicated that the recency of communication between users (number of days since last communication) is the most predictive variable for the estimation of tie strength, but the addition of other variables can significantly improve the accuracy of the results. The same model has also been applied to a different social medium (i.e. Twitter), with accurate results in the prediction of tie strength through the use of relational variables [73].

Regression models using tie strength as a latent variable have been proposed by Khosravi et al. [74] (for Cloob – an Iranian social network) and by Xiang et al. [75] for Facebook. In particular, the model in [75] attempts to represent tie strength as a combination of interaction and profile variables. A limitation of this approach is that it does not use explicit evaluations of tie strength, but, instead, tie strength is a latent variable, and the accuracy in the prediction cannot be directly tested.

The work done by Jones et al. [76] is aimed at automatically classifying strong and weak ties in Facebook. The results indicate that the frequency of online interactions is predictive of strong ties, and that attributes derived from profile data are less useful for the identification of strong relationships. The limitation of this work is that tie strength is treated as a binary variable, without considering possible intermediate values between 'strong' and 'weak'.

Wu et al. [77] demonstrate the possibility of correctly estimating different values of tie strength for professional and personal social relationships from OSN data. They analysed information extracted from Beehive, a social network site developed by IBM for its employees, and they ask some users to rate their friendships both in the private and professional spheres. The results indicate that the level of direct interaction is predictor of personal tie strength, but not of professional tie strength.

Although the work presented in this section confirms the possibility of estimating tie strength through OSN data, a detailed characterisation of the correlation and representativeness of a large number of interaction variables and tie strength in OSN, and in Facebook in particular, is still missing. In the following sections, we present our contribution to this field. Specifically, we summarise the results of the analyses we conducted on Facebook to characterise the composition of tie strength in online environments, initially presented in [78–80].

### 3.2.2 Facebook Data and Analysis Methodology

The kinds of interaction information needed to derive tie strength models are subject to Facebook privacy constraints. Consequently, this information is typically not available in the datasets publicly available for research. For this reason, we analysed data through a dedicated Facebook application called Facebook Analyzer (FBA) [78]. FBA analyses information related to the logged-in users obtainable through Facebook Application Programming

Interfaces (APIs). The only limitation of FBA is the need for specific permission from the users before analysing their data.

Using FBA, we also analysed explicit evaluations of tie strength from the users, in a similar way to the application presented in [72]. Specifically, we asked the participants to evaluate all their friendships, by answering the following question: 'How do you rate, with a value between 0 and 100, the social relationship between you and this person in Facebook?' They were asked to evaluate social relationships considering only their activity and interactions in Facebook, thus disregarding any other interactions occurring with their friends offline.

For these purposes, we sampled 30 people, of whom 28 evaluated all their Facebook friends through FBA. We studied a total of 7103 social relationships, for which we analysed all the Facebook variables obtainable through Facebook APIs. This data permits a reasonable analysis of the factors that characterise these virtual relationships, and a well grounded regression analysis to estimate tie strength. Whilst the number of users involved in the experiment may not be sufficient to draw definite conclusions about the properties of ego networks in Facebook as a whole, the number of sampled social relationships is adequate for an analysis of tie strength.

To study the composition of tie strength in Facebook, we identified a set of variables, which we intuitively related to the relationships between users in Facebook (Table 3.1). The rationale behind the selection of these variables was to take a rather broad set of measures describing overall properties of the interactions between users that are intuitively related to the properties of tie strength, and then use statistical analysis to identify the variables that best describe and predict it. For a more complete description of these variables we refer the reader to our previous work [78].

The distribution of the evaluations of tie strength self-reported by the participants and the distributions of all the Facebook interaction variables that we have analysed have a long-tailed distribution, with most of the relationships having a very low value of tie strength, and only a few relationships with high tie strength. As discussed Section 2.2.2, this trend is typical in social networks. The explicit evaluations of tie strength are used as 'ground truth' to understand the impact of the different types of online social interactions on tie strength, and to compare and calibrate the tie strength prediction models. Note that the ultimate goal of the prediction models is

| Table 3.1 Collected Variables in Facebook | |
|---|---|
| No. | Variable |
| 1 | Number of days since last communication |
| 2 | Bidirectional frequency of contact |
| 3 | Number of days since first communication |
| 4 | Frequency of incoming communication |
| 5 | Number of received comments |
| 6 | Frequency of outgoing communication |
| 7 | Number of comments sent |
| 8 | Number of received posts |
| 9 | Number of received private messages |
| 10 | Number of posts sent |
| 11 | Number of likes sent |
| 12 | Number of received likes |
| 13 | Number of friends' pictures in which user appears |
| 14 | Number of fan pages in common |
| 15 | Number of tags on the same objects |
| 16 | Number of groups in common |
| 17 | Number of user's pictures in which friends appear |
| 18 | Number of events in common |
| 19 | Number of private messages sent |

to avoid asking explicit tie strength values. Yet, in order to calibrate the models, explicit tie strength evaluations are essential in this phase.

### 3.2.3 The Composition of Tie Strength in Facebook

As a first step, we used PCA to explore the structure of the nature of the Facebook variables which we selected (as listed in Table 3.1). PCA is a standard technique that extracts, from a set of possibly correlated variables, a set of uncorrelated factors, obtained as linear combinations of the original variables, and constituting the main dimensions of the variables. Further details on the technique which we used for the extraction of the principal factors of the dataset can be found in [78].

The PCA identifies five main factors, which between them explain 65% of the variance in the data. The results obtained by PCA, in terms of factor loadings (i.e. the weights that variables have in the composition of the factor), are reported in Table 3.2. Values in italic represent meaningful variables for the factors (i.e. ones with load $> 0.3$).

**Table 3.2  PCA Factor Loadings**

| Variable | Factor | | | | |
|---|---|---|---|---|---|
| | I | II | III | IV | V |
| 1 | −0.77 | −0.29 | −0.07 | −0.17 | −0.12 |
| 2 | 0.88 | 0.28 | 0.09 | 0.17 | 0.11 |
| 3 | 0.82 | 0.18 | 0.10 | 0.08 | 0.03 |
| 4 | 0.90 | 0.08 | 0.09 | 0.16 | 0.14 |
| 5 | 0.44 | 0.28 | 0.22 | 0.29 | 0.30 |
| 6 | 0.32 | 0.70 | 0.07 | 0.22 | 0.13 |
| 7 | 0.21 | 0.61 | 0.12 | 0.31 | 0.28 |
| 8 | 0.78 | 0.02 | 0.18 | 0.08 | 0.07 |
| 9 | 0.54 | 0.10 | −0.14 | 0.24 | 0.26 |
| 10 | 0.35 | 0.51 | 0.10 | 0.12 | 0.06 |
| 11 | 0.04 | 0.56 | 0.14 | 0.29 | 0.24 |
| 12 | 0.22 | 0.23 | 0.24 | 0.29 | 0.30 |
| 13 | 0.16 | 0.05 | 0.22 | 0.30 | 0.34 |
| 14 | 0.06 | 0.26 | 0.15 | 0.35 | 0.49 |
| 15 | 0.10 | 0.05 | 0.77 | 0.07 | 0.05 |
| 16 | 0.10 | 0.09 | 0.79 | 0.05 | 0.03 |
| 17 | 0.08 | 0.19 | −0.03 | 0.29 | 0.45 |
| 18 | 0.06 | 0.05 | 0.46 | 0.13 | 0.12 |
| 19 | 0.01 | 0.37 | −0.09 | 0.20 | 0.21 |

We provide a characterisation of the physical meaning of each factor, based on the variables that determine it and their factor loadings (see Table 3.2), to give a first broad idea on the nature of the principal dimensions contained in the dataset. Furthermore, we provide a preliminary comparison between the differences of these dimensions and those hypothesised by Granovetter [45].

The first two factors contain all the variables related to the communi-cation between people, such as the *frequency of contact*, the *time since last/first communication*, the *number of likes/posts/messages, etc.* sent or received by egos. We call these factors 'communication factors'. The first factor embodies the incoming communication and the overlap between the incoming and the outgoing communication (i.e. the incoming communica-tion reciprocated by ego). The second factor contains the portion of outgoing communication not already contained in the first factor, that is to say the outgoing communication not reciprocated by alters. The fact that outgoing communication is split between the first two factors is likely to be the reason why they are uncorrelated. In fact, in our dataset, incoming and outgoing communications are not that well correlated ($r = 0.33, p < 0.01$), which confirms previous analyses on this aspect in Facebook [81].

The third factor is a combination of the *number of groups* and *events* in common and the *number of tags on the same objects*. This factor represents how similar two Facebook profiles are and we call it 'social similarity factor'. The last two factors share broadly the same variables and they seem related to the intimacy and the emotional intensity of a relationship since they contain, amongst other variables, the number of pictures in which two users appear together, which is an indication of their emotional affinity.

The tie strength dimensions identified by Granovetter are the following: *time, emotional intensity, intimacy,* and the *reciprocal services* which characterise the tie. The results of our factor analysis broadly indicate that the same dimensions hypothesised by Granovetter can be identified in Facebook. Specifically, the first two Facebook factors are related to the time ego spends for socialising with alters, and indicate the emotional intensity of the relationships. Moreover, the last two Facebook factors indicate both emotional intensity and intimacy. Granovetter's definition does not take into account the social similarity between people, an important factor that emerges from our analysis, but this factor could be a combination of emotional intensity and intimacy. The only factor that is not present in our data is the one concerning reciprocal services. However, in our data, we do not have any direct indication of reciprocal services in Facebook, and the concept of reciprocal services in OSNs is not as intuitive as in offline environments.

### 3.2.4 Models for the Prediction of Tie Strength

In this section, we present a series of tie strength prediction models built from the selected Facebook variables and the tie strength evaluations given by the participants. Before introducing the models, a preliminary correlation analysis between the relational variables and the tie strength values is presented. Then, we introduce the linear regression models for the prediction of tie strength. A linear approach has been adopted for all the models since the aim of this analysis is to keep the model as simple as possible. In addition, the choice has been motivated by the definition of tie strength given by Granovetter, where tie strength is considered to be a (probably) linear combination of social factors.

## Correlation Between Facebook Variables and Tie Strength

We studied the correlation between each variable in the dataset and the evaluations of tie strength provided by the users using the Pearson product-moment correlation coefficient, described in greater detail in [78]. The correlation values, ordered from the highest to the lowest, are reported in Table 3.3. In the table, the $p$-values related to the correlation are omitted, since they all satisfy $p < 0.01$. The variables showing the highest correlation with tie strength are the *number of days since last communication*, the *frequency of contact* (both bidirectional and related to incoming interactions only) and the *number of days since first communication*. The first of these variables, representing the recency of communication, has been used in previous work as an estimator of the frequency of contact between individuals and as an estimate of tie strength [64]. The correlation between Facebook variables and tie strength provides a first indication of the feasibility of the creation of a tie strength prediction model.

| No. | Variable | $r$ |
|---|---|---|
| 1 | Number of days since last communication | −0.56 |
| 2 | Bidirectional frequency of contact | 0.55 |
| 3 | Number of days since first communication | 0.51 |
| 4 | Frequency of incoming communication | 0.50 |
| 5 | Number of received comments | 0.47 |
| 6 | Frequency of outgoing communication | 0.44 |
| 7 | Number of comments sent | 0.43 |
| 8 | Number of received posts | 0.41 |
| 9 | Number of received private messages | 0.34 |
| 10 | Number of posts sent | 0.33 |
| 11 | Number of likes sent | 0.32 |
| 12 | Number of received likes | 0.29 |
| 13 | Number of friends' pictures in which user appears | 0.24 |
| 14 | Number of fan pages in common | 0.20 |
| 15 | Number of tags on the same object | 0.20 |
| 16 | Number of groups in common | 0.20 |
| 17 | Number of ego's pictures in which alters appear | 0.17 |
| 18 | Number of events in common | 0.14 |
| 19 | Number of private messages sent | 0.11 |

Table 3.3 Correlation Between Facebook Variables and Tie Strength of Each Alter as Rated by the Individual Egos

## Model With Uncorrelated Variables

The first family of models created to predict tie strength and to describe further its composition is based on a set of uncorrelated regressors. To build these models we calculated the correlation between all the possible combinations of pairs of variables, and then selected a set of regressors through the iterative procedure described in [78], which guarantees that not too many correlated variables are present in the model (this problem is known as multicollinearity). Using correlation to select the regressors in the models allows us to obtain results that can be easily interpreted and reduces as much as possible the number of regressors of the models. Nevertheless, we also used more adequate methods, such as stepwise regression to select the best combination of regressors in the models, and mixed model regression with ego as a covariate. The accuracy of the models obtained with these methods is of the same order of that found using correlation.

The second model we built uses the same set of uncorrelated regressors of the previous model and, in addition, it includes all the pairwise products between the regressors. Using pairwise products is a standard technique in regression analysis to improve fit by introducing a set of simple non-linear terms. We also considered other benchmark models. In the first of these, we considered the *recency of communication* as the sole regressor, as this is the variable that correlates most with tie strength (see Table 3.3). For completeness, a model with all the variables as regressors is also reported. This model, although suffering from multicollinearity and probably overfitting, represents a reference point for the other models. Another model we considered is a very simple model used as baseline to assess the validity of the other models. It is a constant model which returns the average score of the evaluations used during the training phase for each possible input.

For each model, the standard indices $R^2$ and the estimated standard error are computed. Then, each model is tested on a test set, computing the Root Mean Square Error (*rmse*). $R^2$ (between 0 and 1) tells us how much the model fits the data on tie strength. The estimated standard error is the average value of the error made by the model whilst fitting the training set. The *rmse* (between 0 and 1) measures the average error made by the model during the prediction phase and is calculated comparing the output of the model and the reference values in the test set (i.e. the tie strength explicitly evaluated by the users). For a precise definition of these indices see [78].

| Table 3.4 Statistics of the Regression Models Based on Uncorrelated Variables | | | |
|---|---|---|---|
| Model | $R^2$ | Std. Error | rmse |
| Average value | 0 | 0.211 | 0.219 |
| One regressor | 0.272 | 0.180 | 0.184 |
| Uncorrelated without pairwise product | 0.345 | 0.171 | 0.177 |
| Uncorrelated with pairwise product | 0.350 | 0.170 | 0.177 |
| All regressors | 0.454 | 0.156 | 0.165 |

The results of the models are reported in Table 3.4. The model with only one regressor is able to explain 27.2% of the variance of the tie strength in the dataset, according to its $R^2$. This represents a rather good result, considering that only one variable is used to estimate tie strength, despite the fact that it is likely to be influenced by many different sociological and psychological factors. Note that $R^2$ values around 0.3 are generally considered good results for this kind of analysis [64]. The estimated standard error of the model is equal to 18%. This means that the model, on average, is able to fit the training set with reasonable accuracy. The *rmse* of the model is really close to the estimated standard error. This is a good result, since indicates that the average error made on the test set has the same magnitude as the error made on the training set. Hence, the model seems not to be affected by overfitting and remains valid even when applied to data other than those used to train it. The model with the addition of the other variables that are uncorrelated with the *recency of communication* shows an improvement in terms of all the presented indices. Even if the improvements in terms of estimated standard error and *rmse* are only 0.9% and 0.7%, respectively, the $R^2$ is 7.3% higher than that of the model with just one regressor. The model with the introduction of the pairwise products of the variables does not bring a sufficient increment in terms of $R^2$ and *rmse* to justify its inclusion. Lastly, the model with all the variables as regressors yields the best performance, but, as stated before, it suffers from multicollinearity. Note that all models significantly outperform the basic benchmark (average value).

The results described so far indicate that the models effectively predict tie strength using only a small set of Facebook variables (i.e. 4 in the model with all the selected uncorrelated variables). The first model, with the *number of days since last communication* as the sole regressor, provides good predictive accuracy, confirming that this variable is a good predictor of tie strength. Nevertheless, using additional variables (i.e. the other regressors in the second model) provides significant improvement in model fit.

**Model With PCA Factors**

In addition to the models presented earlier, we also created a model using the PCA factors obtained from the variables. Using the factor scores obtained from PCA, we created three different regression models. The first model uses only the first PCA factor as regressor (the factor with the strongest correlation with tie strength). A second model uses all the five PCA factors, and a third one contains all the factors and their pairwise products.

The $R^2$, the estimated standard error and the *rmse* of the models are reported in Table 3.5. The first model has a noticeably lower value of $R^2$ compared to the other models and the error it makes during prediction is higher (almost 20%). The second model, in contrast, shows a good $R^2$, with a sensible improvement compared to the previous one. Also the *rmse* and the average standard error indicate better performances, not far from the reference model built using all the possible regressors reported in Table 3.4. The third model introduces an additional improvement in terms of $R^2$, but its greater complexity is not supported by a noticeable improvement in terms of prediction accuracy. Hence, the second model turns out to be the best one, since it is simpler than the third one – maintaining a similar $R^2$ at the same time – and has a far better $R^2$ compared to the first model.

**3.2.4.1 Comparison Between the Different Models**

The models described so far have approximately the same predictive power in terms of *rmse* ($M = 0.180$, SD $= 0.010$). This represents a good result, since all the models are able to predict tie strength with an accuracy greater than 80%. The model using only recency of contacts is the simplest one, and generally performs very well. The model achieving the best performance is the one with all PCA factors. Its performances are equivalent to the linear model using all regressors, but does not suffer from multicollinearity. A

**Table 3.5 Statistics of the Regression Models With PCA Factors**

| Model | $R^2$ | Residual Std. Error | *rmse* |
|---|---|---|---|
| First PCA factor | 0.193 | 0.189 | 0.198 |
| PCA factors I–V | 0.404 | 0.163 | 0.171 |
| PCA factors I–V + pairwise products | 0.423 | 0.161 | 0.171 |

drawback of this model is that it needs all relational variables. In cases where this is not feasible, the model using the four uncorrelated variables is a very good trade-off. It is not much more complex than the one using only one regressor (*recency of contact*), and is able to provide higher $R^2$ and lower *rmse*, although it does not reach the performance of the model with all PCA factors.

It is noteworthy that the most important variable for tie strength prediction remains the *time since last contact* in all the models. The results also confirm that this variable is a good estimator of the frequency of contact, since it has a very high correlation with the *bidirectional frequency of contact* ($r = -0.86, p < 0.01$). Moreover, it also represents a large portion of the first PCA factor. The *time since last contact* is also really simple to obtain from Facebook and the model that uses only this variable as predictor requires only a small amount of information. In fact, it is sufficient to observe only the last communication record and not the whole history of interactions between the users to obtain the time at which the last contact between two online users occurred.

## 3.3 THE STRUCTURE OF EGO NETWORKS IN FACEBOOK

In this section, we present an analysis on the structure of ego networks in Facebook that we initially introduced in [82, 83]. The analysis is aimed at assessing the presence in Facebook ego networks of the hierarchical structure of layers found in offline social networks, described in Section 2.4.1. Firstly, in Section 3.3.1, we give a detailed description of the Facebook datasets we used for the analysis. Then, in Section 3.3.2, we present the methodology we used in the analysis and the results we obtained. Finally, we discuss the results and their implications in Section 3.3.4.

### 3.3.1 Large-Scale Datasets for Online Ego Networks Analysis

For the analysis, we use two large-scale Facebook datasets containing communication traces between online users. The datasets, which are different from the data described in Section 3.2.2, contain less detailed information about all the different types of interactions between users, and cannot be used for an accurate analysis of tie strength in Facebook. Nonetheless, they contain enough information about social interactions between users to analyse ego-network structure. Specifically, from the communication traces in the datasets it is possible to extract the contact frequency between users, and this is used as an estimation of tie strength, as supported by the results presented in Section 3.2. Compared to the data described in Section 3.2, the datasets used here contain many more users and the dyadic relationships between them. This allowed us to obtain significant results about the properties of ego networks in Facebook for a much larger sample.

The datasets (for simplicity, we will call them Dataset 1 and Dataset 2) were downloaded from Facebook before 2009, when the privacy policies were still not too restrictive, and the amount of publicly available information obtainable from Facebook APIs was sufficient for reconstructing a large portion of the entire social network.

### 3.3.1.1 Dataset 1

Dataset 1 [84] was downloaded by Wilson et al. [27] using a crawling agent that obtained the complete public profile information (including personal information and the list of Facebook friends), and the Facebook wall data of a set of users in a large regional network of Facebook. The dataset covers the time span from the start of Facebook in September 2004 until April 2008. The dataset consists of more than 3 million nodes and more than 23 million edges (social links identified by cross-postings), with an edge representing a Facebook friendship. As explained in [27], it represents only a sub-sample of a Facebook regional network, in terms of downloaded Facebook profiles ($\sim$56%) and their Facebook friendships ($\sim$37%). Other analyses on Facebook ego network structure have been conducted using this dataset [82], but here we report a more refined analysis of the dataset, which allows us to obtain more accurate results about the size and the composition of ego network layers.

The 44% of profiles in the regional network that have not been downloaded were profiles with restrictive privacy settings or users disconnected from the giant component. Despite the high number of missing profiles, some of their data are still present in the dataset. In fact, if a public profile of a user A was connected to a non-public profile B, the posts sent from B to A were still visible in A's Facebook wall. Moreover, B would appear in the friend list of A. Therefore, information exchanged on links from non-public profiles to public profiles is available. We miss information related to posts (i) from public profiles (node A in our example) to non-public profiles (node

B) and (ii) between non-public profiles. In addition, the dataset only reports the ID of users, without indicating whether their profile is public or private. We discuss below how we estimate missing traffic related to (i). As for (ii), the amount of data collected for non-public profiles is usually lower than that of public profiles since the only communication traces available for them are those indirectly appearing inside the walls of the set of their friends which are public users. For this reason, most private profiles appear in the dataset as users with low Facebook usage, and most of them are discarded during our pre-processing phase. Given this, we argue that missing information about their mutual interaction is not particularly problematic for our purposes. Hence, we reasonably assume that, despite not containing all the possible communication records between users in the regional network, the dataset is still a valid representation of Facebook social network for the purpose of ego network analysis.

We managed to partly reconstruct missing information with respect to point (i) above, as follows. We cannot tell from the dataset itself which profiles are public and which are not because, for a given friendship relationship, the dataset only reports the number of (undirected) interactions (posts or photo comments) that occurred, and not the properties of the profiles of the users involved, or the detailed interaction log. Therefore, we do not know for which links in the dataset we are missing interactions in one of the two directions. The only information we have is the percentage of non-public profiles, that is, 44%. For this reason, we have selected randomly 44% of nodes, and assumed that those are associated with the non-public profiles. We have doubled the number of interactions on all the links of the ego networks of those nodes. This corresponds to assuming that these relationships are perfectly bi-directional, and the (unknown) amount of interaction from public to non-public profiles is the same as the (known) amount of interaction in the opposite direction. We can expect that this process makes our results for internal layers accurate and less precise for external layers, for the following reasons. First, it is known that bi-directionality becomes stronger and stronger as relationships become more and more intimate. Therefore, doubling interactions on strong relationships is very reasonable, whilst it is less accurate for weak ties. In addition, this process does not modify interactions over links for which we have no interactions in the dataset. Hence, after adjusting the amount of interactions there may still be some relationships for which we incorrectly consider no interactions, that is relationships for which real interactions have occurred only in the direction from a public to a non-public profile. Such strongly asymmetrical relationships are typically known to belong to the most external layers of the ego networks. The net expected effect is, therefore, that the size of internal layers is precise, whilst that of external layers may be underestimated.

The dataset provides an approximate measure of time in so far as the data are coded into four time periods (postings or contacts within the last month, last 6 months, last year and the entire duration of the link). From these time periods, we create 4 time-based non-inclusive windows $w_k$ ($k \in 1, 2, 3, 4$), with $w_1$ indicating the time interval between the download and 1 month before the download (last month), $w_2$ between 1 month before the download and 6 months before the download (last 6 months) and so on.

We define as 'active' all the relationships that have at least one interaction in any of the windows $w_k$. For each link, we use the difference between the number of interactions made in the different temporal windows to compute contact frequency, and we interpret this as an estimate of the intimacy of the relationship. A complete description of the methodology we used to obtain the contact frequency of the relationships in the dataset can be found in [82].

For the analysis we consider only egos with an average of more than 10 interactions per month, thus selecting 'socially active people' since they are particularly relevant for our analysis, and discard inactive profiles. In addition, for each ego, we removed social relationships whose frequency of interaction is lower than one message per year. This is to avoid considering people in whom the ego does not invest some minimum amount of time and cognitive resources. We choose the limit as one message per year in accordance with the definition of active network in offline ego networks [64]. In this way, we can avoid considering ego network layers external to the active network, which still lack a precise definition, and whose properties are not completely known. The resulting dataset is composed of 130,338 egos with 5,289,910 active edges (i.e. friendships with at least one interaction). Note that, to extract ego networks from the datasets, we first create a series of sets each of which contains all the social relationships of a user.

### 3.3.1.2 Dataset 2
Dataset 2, similarly to Dataset 1, was downloaded in 2009 exploiting the Facebook regional network feature [85]. It represents the Facebook regional network of New Orleans and it has been obtained through a crawling agent

similar to the one created for downloading Dataset 1. Compared to the first dataset, Dataset 2 represents a smaller regional network (90,269 nodes and 3,646,662 social links), but the data it contains are much more detailed. Specifically, for each public profile visited by the crawler, the dataset reports the list of its Facebook friends and the list of wall posts received by the user from her friends, with the timestamp indicating the time at which the interaction occurred. In contrast to Dataset 1, where it was not possible to identify the set of public profiles, here we know exactly which public profile has been visited by the crawling agent, and we can perform a more precise analysis, taking only public profiles as the egos for our ego network analysis. For these profiles, we know the exact size of the ego network (as we know the entire set of friends), and we can reconstruct almost entirely information about interactions, as described below. After selecting public profiles and all their social interactions, we obtain a dataset containing 60,290 nodes (egos) with a total of 1,545,686 social relationships. The data collected for each ego represents her Facebook wall. For this reason, they contain only the communications received by the users from her friends. For friends with public profiles, we can complement the information available on the ego's wall and reconstruct the exact number of mutual interactions by analysing the friend's wall, where posts and photo comments made by ego are available. As in the case of Dataset 1, we doubled the number of interactions available on the ego's wall for friends with private profiles (which may result in approximations primarily in external layers of ego networks, as discussed above).

Even though Dataset 2 contains more accurate information than Dataset 1, the larger size of the latter makes it a more significant sample of the entire Facebook network. The main purpose of the analysis on Dataset 2 is to validate results obtained from Dataset 1. To this end, we used Dataset 2 also to validate the reconstruction methodology applied to Dataset 1.

We calculate the frequency of contact between users in Dataset 2 as the number of interactions between them divided by the duration of their relationship, estimated as the time since their first contact, considered from the time of the download. In contrast to Dataset 1, here we have precise information about the duration of the relationships.

Also in this case, we select 'socially active users', taking into consideration only users who had at least 10 interactions per month. After this pre-processing, the dataset contains 5761 egos and 107,029 social relationships.

## 3.3.2 The Layered Structure of Ego Networks in Facebook

To analyse the structure of ego networks in OSNs, for each ego network, we apply cluster analysis to the values of contact frequency with each alter. In this way, alters with similar contact frequency are grouped together in the same cluster. The clusters we obtain can be seen as the external parts of the circles in the ego network model (i.e. not considering the nested circles), where alters are also grouped according to their contact frequency. For the analysis, we use two different clustering techniques, $k$-means (a partitioning clustering technique) and DBSCAN (a density-based clustering technique), to search for a layered structure in the ego networks of Facebook.

Partitioning clustering algorithms start with a set of objects and divide the data space into $k$ clusters so that the objects inside a cluster are more similar to each other than objects in other clusters. For each ego network, we order alters in a one-dimensional space by contact frequency with the ego, and search for clusters in this one-dimensional space using the technique described in [86]. The $k$-means algorithm enables us to find the optimal clustering configuration for one-dimensional data spaces.

The $k$-means approach involves partitioning the data space into $k$ different clusters of objects, so that the sum of squared Euclidean distances between the centre of each cluster and the individual objects inside that cluster is minimised. The goodness of fit of $k$-means algorithm is often expressed in terms of variance explained $VAR_{exp}$, defined as follows:

$$VAR_{exp} = \frac{SS_{TOT} - \sum_{i=1}^{k} SS_i}{SS_{TOT}} \tag{3.1}$$

where $SS_{TOT}$ is the total sum of squares in the data space and $SS_i$ is the within sum of squares of the $i$th cluster. $VAR_{exp}$ is analogous to the conventional coefficient of determination $R^2$, which ranges between 0 and 1.

We apply $k$-means in two different ways. On the one hand, we want to find the typical number of clusters in the ego networks, as we want to verify if online ego networks show a layered structure with a number of layers similar to that found in offline social networks. To do so, we apply $k$-means to each ego network with different values of $k$. However, since $VAR_{exp}$ will always be maximised when $k$ is equal to the number of objects in the data space, we need an algorithm to avoid this over-fitting problem in order to discover the optimal number of clusters in our ego networks. To do this, we calculate the Akaike Information Criterion (AIC) index of the model for each $k$-means configuration, and, by varying $k$ from 1 to 20, take the value of $k$ that minimises the value of AIC. This value is the optimal number of clusters $k^*$ for the ego network. This is a standard approach for the analysis of the optimal number of clusters in a data space [87].

The probability density functions of the values of $k^*$ that we obtained from the ego networks in the two Facebook datasets are shown in Figure 3.1. The distributions show a marked peak around $k^* = 4$. For Dataset 1, the ego networks have an average optimal number of clusters equal to 4.35 (with median 4), and Dataset 2 has an average optimal number of clusters of 4.10 (with median 4). These results are compatible with the properties of ego networks found in offline environments, in which the typical number of layers is 4.

The AIC is a measure representing the relative quality of the clustering configurations. It is useful to find the optimal number of clusters in the data, but it does not indicate a direct measure of the goodness of a single configuration since it only provides a ranking between possible configurations. For this reason, even if we are able to identify the optimal number of clusters in the contact frequency of an ego network by using the AIC, we do not know if the data are effectively centred on the centroids of the clusters or not. To measure how well the data are clustered, we calculate the Silhouette statistics for each optimal configuration. The Silhouette of

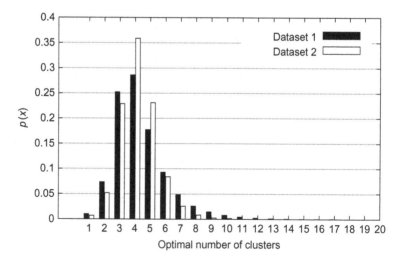

*Figure 3.1 Optimal number of clusters found by k-means using AIC as the optimisation criterion for the ego networks in the two Facebook datasets.*

a single data point $x$, $s(x)$, measures the extent to which $x$ is appropriately assigned to its cluster. Specifically, given $a(x)$, the average distance between $x$ and all the other points in the same cluster, and $b(x)$, the minimum amongst the average distances between $x$ and elements in each of the other clusters, $s(x)$ is defined as follows:

$$s(x) = \frac{b(x) - a(x)}{\max\{a(x), b(x)\}} \tag{3.2}$$

The average value of $s(x)$ for all $x$ in the data space indicates the appropriateness of the clustering configuration. The value of $s(x)$ ranges between $-1$ and $1$. Values close to $-1$ indicate that the points could have been assigned to the wrong clusters. On the other hand, values close to $0$ indicate that the data are poorly clustered and thus uniformly distributed around centroids. In this case, the clustering configuration could be suboptimal, or the data could not be naturally grouped into clusters. Lastly, values of $s(x)$ close to $1$ indicate that the data are appropriately clustered, and densely distributed around centroids. If the best clustering configuration identified through the AIC is associated with a value of $s(x)$ close to $1$, the data are naturally divided into groups that are effectively matched by the obtained clusters.

The average Silhouette value for the best configurations associated with the optimal number of clusters for each ego network is 0.670 for Dataset 1, and 0.678 for Dataset 2. These values indicate that the data are appropriately clustered, and that the identified clusters are not fictitious.

The distribution of the values of $k^*$ is shown in Figure 3.1. Since the modal value, the average value and the median are close to 4 for both datasets, we apply $k$-means with $k = 4$ on all the ego networks in the datasets to be able to calculate the average size and contact frequency of the layers, and to compare them with the results found offline. We report the respective values for each layer in Table 3.6. Note that the layer sizes obtained by cluster analysis are the numbers of individuals in each annulus, not the cumulative number of individuals in successive layers as defined in the literature. To obtain the layers equivalent to those defined in the literature, we nest the clusters, obtaining a series of concentric layers.

### 3.3.3 Validation
We performed a double validation on the results presented in Table 3.6. On the one hand, we checked the results obtained with $k$-means using

| Table 3.6 Properties of Ego Network Layers in Facebook | | | | | |
|---|---|---|---|---|---|
| Layer | 0 | 1 | 2 | 3 | 4 |
| *Offline networks* | | | | | |
| Size | ? | 5 | 15 | 50 | 150 |
| Contact freq. | ? | 48 | 12 | 2 | 1 |
| *Dataset 1* | | | | | |
| Size (*k*-means) | $1.68 \pm 0.01$ | $5.28 \pm 0.02$ | $14.92 \pm 0.06$ | $40.93 \pm 0.20$ | – |
| Contact freq. | $77.36 \pm 0.77$ | $30.28 \pm 0.24$ | $11.15 \pm 0.07$ | $2.53 \pm 0.01$ | – |
| *Dataset 2* | | | | | |
| Size (*k*-means) | $1.53 \pm 0.03$ | $4.34 \pm 0.09$ | $10.72 \pm 0.23$ | $26.99 \pm 0.61$ | – |
| Contact freq. | $58.54 \pm 2.62$ | $22.19 \pm 0.74$ | $7.93 \pm 0.23$ | $1.37 \pm 0.04$ | – |

a different and more complex clustering algorithm, particularly suited in case of irregular density of the data. On the other hand, we validated the methodology we used to reconstruct missing information in Dataset 1, by applying the same methodology on Dataset 2, and then studying the size and contact frequency of the resulting ego network layers. As far as the first point is concerned, $k$-means may be affected by the presence of noisy data (i.e. points in the data space with a very low density compared to the other points around them). Noise can affect a $k$-means analysis in two different ways: (i) the presence of noisy points between two adjacent clusters might cause the algorithm to treat them all as a single cluster instead of two (the so-called 'single link effect' [88]), whilst (ii) the presence of a large number of noisy points in the data set could lead to the detection of more clusters than really exist. To ensure that noisy points do not adversely influence the outcome, we compare the results with the DBSCAN density-based clustering algorithm [89]. In contrast to partitioning clustering, density-based clustering algorithms are able to identify clusters in a space of objects with areas with different densities [88]. DBSCAN defines two parameters, $\epsilon$ and MinPts, and any object with more than MinPts neighbours within a distance $\epsilon$ is defined as a core object. A cluster is made up by a group of core objects (adjacent elements separated by less than $\epsilon$) and by the 'border objects' of the cluster (termed 'non-core objects') linked to a core object at a distance less than $\epsilon$. For a more formal definition of density-based clusters, see [89]. Points with less than MinPts neighbours within a distance $\epsilon$ that are not border objects are considered noise by DBSCAN, and they are excluded from the clusters. We iterate DBSCAN decreasing the value of $\epsilon$ until we find a number of clusters equal to the number of clusters obtained by $k$-means. Hence, by comparing the results of $k$-means and DBSCAN in terms of cluster size, we can verify that the former are valid and not influenced by noisy points. To allow noisy data to be identified by the iterative DBSCAN procedure, we set the parameter MinPts $= 2$. In this way, isolated points are excluded from the clusters.

We checked the sizes of the ego network layers using the density-based clustering algorithm DBSCAN to control for noisy points, and the results, as reported in Table 3.7, are very similar to those found by $k$-means. Specifically, in both datasets, the last layer found by DBSCAN differs for a maximum of about three elements from the results of $k$-means. Also the results of the remaining layers for $k$-means and DBSCAN are very similar, confirming that $k$-means, despite its simplicity, is able to identify the correct clusters in the ego networks data.

In Table 3.8, we report the results of the analysis on Dataset 2 aimed at validating the procedure used on Dataset 1 to reconstruct missing data about the communication from public to private user profiles. To perform this analysis, we proceeded as follows. In Dataset 2, 58% of the nodes are non-public. We apply the same reconstruction methodology used in Dataset 1, by sampling 58% of nodes from the entire dataset, and doubling the interactions for all their links. Then, we repeat the analysis to characterise ego network structures, and compare the results obtained with the reconstruction methodology applied to Dataset 2.

The sizes of the ego network layers in Dataset 2 and in the same dataset pre-processed with the reconstruction procedure used for Dataset 1 are really similar. The minimum contact frequencies of the layers, when using the reconstruction procedure of Dataset 1, are slightly higher than the correct

**Table 3.7 Size of Ego Network Layers Found by DBSCAN**

| Layer | 0 | 1 | 2 | 3 | 4 |
|---|---|---|---|---|---|
| Dataset 1 | $2.87 \pm 0.01$ | $7.34 \pm 0.03$ | $18.86 \pm 0.09$ | $37.53 \pm 0.20$ | – |
| Dataset 2 | $2.57 \pm 0.05$ | $5.86 \pm 0.10$ | $10.65 \pm 0.20$ | $27.02 \pm 0.69$ | – |

**Table 3.8 Properties of Ego Network Layers of Dataset 2 With Reconstruction**

| Layer | 0 | 1 | 2 | 3 | 4 |
|---|---|---|---|---|---|
| Size ($k$-means) | $1.50 \pm 0.03$ | $4.22 \pm 0.07$ | $10.13 \pm 0.17$ | $25.02 \pm 0.48$ | – |
| Contact freq. | $72.95 \pm 2.62$ | $27.90 \pm 0.73$ | $10.35 \pm 0.24$ | $1.83 \pm 0.05$ | – |

ones, but nonetheless similar to those found in Dataset 1. This seems to indicate that the results of Dataset 1, in terms of minimum contact frequency, could be slightly overestimated, and so could be more similar to those found for Dataset 2.

### 3.3.4 Discussion

We denote as layers 1–4 the layers in the conventional ego network model obtained with offline datasets. The characteristic sizes and contact frequencies of each of these layers in offline ego-centric personal social networks has been derived from [58]. In the tables, we matched the layers which we have found in Facebook with those found offline according to their size and contact frequency. In addition, however, we observe an additional inner circle, that we denote as layer 0 in the tables.

Table 3.6 also gives, for the two datasets, the average value of the minimum contact frequency of the layers (i.e. the lower frequency of the layers, indicating the boundaries between them). The frequencies are expressed in number of messages sent by the ego per year. These suggest that in Facebook individual alters are contacted approximately at least every 5 days for layer 0, at least every 12 days for layer 1, at least once a month for layer 2 and at least once every 6 months for layer 3. For layers 1–3, these values are comparable with those obtained for the first three layers (i.e. support clique, sympathy group and affinity group) in offline networks [61].

Our analysis of Facebook communication datasets confirms the layered structure found in offline social networks, in terms of number of layers, size and typical contact frequency. For both the online datasets, the scaling ratio for the various layers identified by the analysis, and the respective sizes of these layers, are extremely close to those observed in offline networks [58, 64, 65]. Furthermore, we observe an inner circle (layer 0 in the tables) that is not visible in offline ego networks. This circle contains very close friends to the ego, whom we can identify as 'intimates' as they are contacted very often. Typically, this layer consists of just one or two alters, who are likely to be a partner and/or a best friend. In terms of size, this layer fits perfectly into the scaling pattern of the hierarchical structure of the ego network model. Its presence is perhaps not too surprising, and, in fact, it had been already hypothesised by extrapolation from the scaling pattern of the nested structure of offline social networks. The fact that this layer had previously not been noted in offline ego networks can be explained by the lack of sufficiently detailed data on the frequency of interactions in these offline datasets.

The sizes of the ego networks for the two Facebook datasets are smaller than the total size of conventional offline ego networks (where the total network size is typically about 150 alters [63, 64]). In our Facebook dataset, the outermost network layer present in offline networks seems to be completely missing. This is, perhaps, not too surprising, since the outermost (150) layer in offline networks corresponds to people who are contacted only about once a year. Early Facebook users (remember that datasets were collected in 2009, when Facebook was still new and yet to start its exponentially increasing diffusion) were not forced into 'friending' complete strangers and, instead, typically only sought out people they knew. Moreover, the outermost network layer is heavily populated by members of the extended family [61] – precisely the people who most early Facebook users were probably unlikely to connect to.

## 3.4 CHAPTER SUMMARY AND DISCUSSION

In this chapter, we presented a detailed overview of tie strength and the structure of ego networks in Facebook. We started from the analysis of the factors underlying tie strength in Facebook, comparing them to the tie strength dimensions in the definition by Granovetter. Then, we presented a series of models for the prediction of tie strength using Facebook interaction variables, and we compared them in terms of predictive power and goodness of fit. Having shown that contact frequency is a good indicator of tie strength, we use two Facebook datasets reporting contact frequency information to study the structural properties of ego networks in Facebook, through an analysis aimed at assessing the presence in Facebook ego networks of the layered structure of the ego networks found in offline environments. Our results indicate that OSNs show the same hierarchical structure observed in offline social networks, but in OSNs we have identified a new inner layer, layer 0, that was only hypothesised in offline social networks. To summarise, the main 'take home messages' of the chapter are as follows.

### Modelling Tie Strength in Facebook

Tie strength can be accurately estimated with social interaction data collected from OSNs. This is supported, firstly, by the fact that the principal factors extracted from variables of social interaction in Facebook are compatible with the tie strength dimensions in the definition given by Granovetter. In addition, the predictive models we created show good accuracy in their estimations. The results confirm that recency of communication and contact frequency (embodying both the intensity and the time spent in a relationship) are the best predictors of tie strength in Facebook. A simple model using the former variable (the one that correlates best with an explicit index of tie strength) as the sole regressor yields sufficiently accurate results to be acceptable. Whilst more complex models could lead to an improvement in accuracy, they require much more information from Facebook of a kind that is often unavailable in large-scale datasets publicly available for research.

## The Structure of Ego Networks in Facebook

Facebook ego networks show a hierarchical structure very similar to the one found in offline ego networks. Specifically, Facebook and offline ego networks have a similar layered structure, with compatible properties in terms of size and contact frequency. Facebook also shows an additional inner circle that fits perfectly in the hierarchy of the layers. This layer is typically composed of just one or two members with very high contact frequency with the ego.

# CHAPTER 4

# The Structure of Ego Networks in Twitter

## 4.1 INTRODUCTION

To investigate the structural properties of Twitter ego networks, we present an analysis on a detailed communication dataset, which we downloaded from Twitter. The uniqueness of the dataset is that it contains information about the complete history of communication of a large number of users in Twitter, and for each exchanged message it reports the timestamp related to its creation. This allowed us to carry out a detailed analysis of the structural properties of ego networks in Twitter. The analysis (initially reported in [83, 90]) is similar to the one performed on Facebook, presented in Chapter 3, and uses the same methodology. The rest of the chapter is structured as follows. In Section 4.2, we describe the dataset. Then, in Section 4.3, we present the structural analysis of the ego networks extracted from the dataset.

## 4.2 DATASET FOR THE ANALYSIS OF TWITTER EGO NETWORKS

We downloaded a large sample of Twitter communication data which we used to build a set of ego networks. We collected data regarding the profile of Twitter users (e.g. username, picture, time zone), the list of their *followers* and *following*, and a complete history of their tweets (up to 3200 tweets per user due to the restrictions imposed by the Application Programming Interface – (API)). For each tweet we obtained its textual content, including the metadata of hashtags, mentions, reply tags and URLs. Notably, we have also collected the timestamp indicating the creation time of each downloaded tweet. This allowed us to obtain an accurate measure of the contact frequency between users, which we used to estimate tie strength and to analyse the structural properties of ego networks.

To obtain a large-scale dataset, we crawled Twitter from November 2012 to March 2013, downloading 2,428,647 complete user profiles. The crawler uses Twitter REST API to collect the data from Twitter. It starts from an initial node and follows links between users to build a network of connected profiles. We started from a very popular user, so that we could immediately have a large sample of other users at the first step of the process. The crawler uses the *following/followers* lists and the content of directed messages (i.e. replies and mentions) to identify new profiles to download.

From the data we downloaded, we built an ego network for each profile. To do so, we firstly defined a measure of the strength of social links between users in Twitter. We say that a social relationship exists between two users, A and B, if A has sent at least a tweet with a *reply* or a *mention* tag to B. This definition of social relationship is associated with directed communication between individuals, and involves thus a cost in terms of cognitive effort spent for the maintenance of the relationship. As an estimate of the tie strength we used the frequency of replies sent from A to B, since replies are usually associated with threads of communications, and are more representative of bi-directional interactions than mentions. Moreover, tweets can contain only one reply tag, and for this reason a reply is usually directed to a single person, whilst multiple users can be mentioned at the same time. Mentions are thus less representative of dyadic interaction than replies.

## 4.2.1 Active Lifespan of Twitter Users

The presence of accurate temporal information about the social interactions between users in the dataset allowed us to calculate the 'active lifespan' of the users, that we define as the period of time over which each profile actively sent tweets. The active lifespan of a user starts with her first tweet and ends with her last tweet. To make the definition of active lifespan more clear, let us consider the following example. If a profile had been created 4 years before the download, but the user associated with the profile sent tweets only during the first year and then stopped using Twitter (at least for sending tweets), the resulting active lifespan of the profile is 1 year. The shape of the distribution of the active lifespan of the egos in the dataset (Figure 4.1) indicates that most of the profiles have very short activity on Twitter. However, the long tail indicates that we were able to obtain profiles with a tweet history of up to almost 7 years (i.e. the complete tweet history of some of the oldest profiles in Twitter as of 2013). Moreover, we found that the users who use Twitter for interacting with others and maintaining their social relationships (which we will define in Section 4.2.2 as 'socially relevant users') rarely generate more than 3200 tweets, and most of the profiles exceeding the limit are generally public figures, news brokers, spammers or other kinds of profiles, that, as we explain below, we do not consider in our analysis. The small peak in the distribution between 1200 and 1400 days could be ascribed to the presence of the limit of 3200

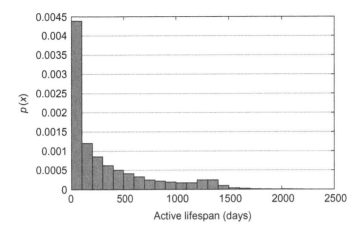

*Figure 4.1 Distribution of active lifespan of Twitter ego networks.*

tweets per user that prevented us from obtaining the complete active lifespan of some of the downloaded profiles. Despite this, the number of profiles affected by this problem is very low and their (last) 3200 tweets are in any case a significant sample to describe their social behaviour. For this reason, the dataset we collected is well suited for our analysis.

Since our analysis is focussed on the social activity of the users in Twitter, we think that measuring the duration of a Twitter account using its active lifespan is appropriate for this work. Of course, some of the users in Twitter could be lurkers, not actively investing their resources in the maintenance of their social relationships. Since we are interested in the analysis of social relationships actively maintained over time through directed communications (the active network in the ego network model), we are not interested in lurking-only users, as they do not actively interact with other people. That said, as has been pointed out by Muller et al. [91], there is not a sharp separation between lurkers and active users since all users alternate between lurking and active behaviour when using social-oriented virtual environments. For this reason, we think that focussing on directed communications is sufficient to capture the social behaviour of the different types of users in Twitter.

## 4.2.2 Socially Relevant Users in Twitter

In contrast to Facebook and other online social networking services, Twitter is designed for heterogeneous types of users. In fact, in addition to accounts used by people mainly to communicate and maintain their social relationships with others (hereafter referred to as *socially relevant users*), in Twitter there are accounts representing companies, public figures, news broadcasters, bloggers and many others, including spammers and bots.

Since we are interested in characterising social aspects of human relationships in online environments, we aim to analyse only socially relevant users, discarding the other types. To do so, we implemented an automatic procedure to divide Twitter accounts in two classes labelled 'socially relevant users' and 'others', respectively. The method we used is similar to that proposed in [92], where the authors present a supervised learning approach to classify Twitter accounts into four different categories (i.e. organisations, journalists/bloggers, ordinary individuals and others). We manually classified a sample of 500 accounts, randomly drawn from the dataset, and used this classification to train a support vector machine (SVM) [93]. This SVM uses a set of 115 variables we extracted from the Twitter dataset: 15 of these related to the user's profile (e.g. number of tweets, number of following and followers, account lifespan) and the remaining 100 were extracted from the user's timeline (e.g. percentage of mentions, replies and retweets, average tweets length, number of tweets made using external applications).

To test the generality of the SVM (i.e. the ability to categorise correctly new examples that differ from those used for training) we took 10 random sub-samples of the training set, each of which contains 80% of the entries, keeping the remaining 20% for testing. Then, we applied the same methodology used to create the SVM generated from the entire training set on the 10 sub-samples. The average accuracy of these SVMs can be seen as an estimate of the accuracy of the SVM derived from the complete training set. Specifically, we calculated the *accuracy* index, defined as the rate of correct classifications, and the *false positives rate*, where false positives are accounts wrongly assigned to the 'socially relevant users' class. In our analysis we considered only 'socially relevant users', thus it is particularly important to minimise the false positive rate. Specifically, false negatives are 'socially relevant users' with behaviour similar to the subjects in the 'others' class. For this reason, we considered them as outliers, since our analysis is focused on Twitter average users. Minimising the false negative rate is also important but less critical, as false negatives merely result in a reduction of the number of users on which we base our analysis.

The average accuracy of the SVM is equal to $0.813 \pm 0.024$ and the average false positives rate is $0.083 \pm 0.012$ (intervals represent 95%

confidence intervals). Although this result could be improved using a larger training set, it is comparable with the results in [92] and is sufficient to give us confidence in drawing inferences about human behaviour within the Twitter environment based on only a very small proportion of crawled accounts.

After applying the SVM to the dataset, we classified 1,653,155 socially relevant users – about 68% of the total number of users in the dataset. As in the case of Facebook datasets, we select only the users who sent their first tweet at least 6 months before the download, and with a minimum of 10 replies sent in total to their alters, so as to discard accounts that are not active enough and, for this reason, are not representative of the social activity of the people behind them. We also discard social relationships started less than 1 month before the download, to avoid the bias due to the initial higher level of communication typical of such relationships [27]. Moreover, we discard all the profiles that have not sent any tweets (i.e. with null active lifespan), reducing the number of profiles to 1,187,105.

The statistics for the selected socially relevant users are reported in Table 4.1. The mean active lifespan of the selected users in the dataset (i.e. 'duration' in the table) is approximately 320 days. This indicates that, on average, we captured almost a full year of communication for each user and this is more than sufficient for conducting an analysis on the evolution over time of social relationships and ego networks. Another interesting property of the dataset is that replies and mentions account for about 39% of the total number of tweets made by socially relevant users in Twitter. This means that the amount of communication data we can use for the definition of social relationships and tie strength is significant. Nonetheless, undirected messages account for the largest component of the

| Table 4.1 Twitter Dataset Statistics | |
|---|---|
| Variable | Mean Value (With CI) |
| Duration (days) | 321.846 (0.628) |
| Replies | 208.923 (0.609) |
| Mentions | 103.882 (0.459) |
| Retweets | 151.492 (0.496) |
| Plain text tweets | 280.037 (0.773) |
| Tweets with URLs | 4.813 (0.032) |
| Tweets with hashtags | 56.411 (0.203) |

communication in Twitter. This kind of communication is controlled by a more *public* behaviour compared to directed messages and it should require fewer cognitive resources, since we expect undirected tweets to contain a low value of emotional intensity. Remarkably, undirected tweets containing URLs are less commonly used than the other type of messages (only 4.8 tweets with URLs sent on average by the users in our dataset during their active lifespan). In addition, the low number of tweets with hashtags (56.4 on average) could be ascribed to the fact that Twitter officially introduced hashtags only between 2009 and 2010.

Figure 4.2 shows the distribution of the communication variables in the dataset for the selected users. We separate directed and undirected communications, with the former identifying the explicit intention of the user to mention other users in the messages. In the figure, we label retweets as directed communication, but their nature needs further investigation. In fact, retweets are more similar to undirected tweets, with the exception that they contain the ID of the user that initially generated the message and the IDs of users that retweeted it.

Mentions show a very long tail (note that the scale of the x-axis is different from that in the other graphs), with a maximum of 23,104 mentions. This high number of mentions, that apparently exceeds the limit

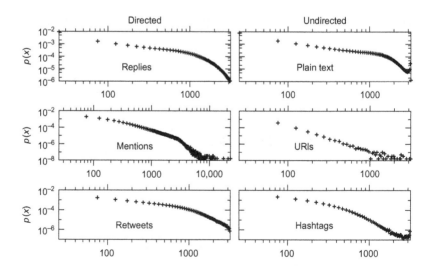

*Figure 4.2 Distribution of the number of tweets divided by type.*

of 3200 tweets per user, is due to the fact that a single tweet can contain more than one mention at the same time.

## 4.3 STRUCTURAL PROPERTIES OF EGO NETWORKS IN TWITTER

In this section, we present an analysis of the structure of the ego networks we extracted from the Twitter dataset. The analysis is aimed at determining whether a layered structure similar to the one found offline and in Facebook is visible also in Twitter ego networks. In Section 4.3.1, we first report an analysis that describes the effect of cognitive and time constraints on Twitter ego networks for socially relevant users, and for the rest of the users in the dataset. Then, in Section 4.3.2, we report the results of the analysis on the structure of ego networks in Twitter. Finally, in Section 4.3.3, we discuss the results, and we compare the properties of the layered structure of ego networks in Twitter and Facebook.

### 4.3.1 Effect of Cognitive Constraints on the Size of Twitter Ego Networks

As a first step in characterising the properties of Twitter ego networks, we studied the average number of replies sent by users to their alters as a function of ego network size. The function is shown in Figure 4.3. We separated the data into the two classes identified in the dataset: 'socially relevant users' and 'others'. The results highlight a clear distinction between the properties of the two classes. Specifically, socially relevant users show

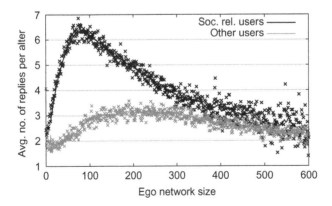

*Figure 4.3 Points represent the average number of replies made by accounts with different number of friends; thick lines are their running averages.*

a higher mean value of replies per alter and a maximum around 80 alters. This could be interpreted as an indication of the effect of the cognitive limits of the human brain on the ability to maintain social relationships in online social networks (OSNs). In fact, the peak of the curve identifies a threshold beyond which the effort dedicated to each social relationship decreases. This is due to the saturation of the available cognitive/time resources that, therefore, have to be distributed over an increasing number of alters. This can be seen as evidence for the social brain hypothesis in Twitter. Notably, the class 'others' shows a more random pattern, with lower average value of replies per alter without any significant discontinuities. This indicates that the accounts belonging to this class are not influenced by cognitive capabilities. In fact, they are often managed by more than one person at the same time or even by non-human agents.

A similar analysis was carried out by Gonçalves et al. [60] using a different Twitter dataset, which yielded a similar peak in the same function as the one shown in Figure 4.3 but spaced somewhere in the interval 100–200 alters. These authors identified this peak as the point of saturation of cognitive resources of the users, and they associated it specifically with Dunbar's number. We would suggest that the peak is indeed an indication of the effect of limited time and cognitive resources in Twitter, but it does not necessarily coincide with Dunbar's number, this being the number of social relationships actively maintained by egos with at least one contact a year. In contrast to [60], our analysis splits users into two classes (loosely interpreted as real vs artificial users), and reveals that these behaved in very different ways. We suggest that combining them causes the flatter distribution of 'artificial users' (i.e. accounts owned by multiple users or non-human agents) to pull the peak for real users further to the right. This makes sense of an important puzzle in the original analysis by [60], namely the implication that Twitter users have their entire social network online in the rather artificial world of Twitter, with presumably no real offline relationships. Our analysis, with a peak at a much lower value (around 80 alters) makes more sense in that it allows users to have a significant (if reduced) number of their social network alters offline in the 'real world'. It may well be plausible that habitual Twitter aficionados involve themselves deeply in the Twitter world precisely because they have fewer offline friends, or that they sacrifice offline friends because so much of their social time is spent online communicating with people they do not know in real life.

## 4.3.2 Ego Network layers in Twitter

We next ran a similar analysis to the one presented for Facebook on the Twitter dataset. Specifically, we used cluster analysis (the same clustering algorithms presented in Section 3.3: *k*-means and DBSCAN) on the values of contact frequency for each ego network extracted from Twitter to group their alters into clusters. We used the Akaike Information Criterion (AIC) to identify the optimal number of clusters of each ego network, and we measured the goodness of the clustering configurations through the Silhouette index. Once we had identified the optimal number of clusters for all the ego networks in the dataset, we applied the clustering algorithms again, this time fixing the number of clusters to the obtained average value. In this way, we obtain a set of layers by nesting the obtained clusters as was done for Facebook. Then, we can calculate the properties of these layers (i.e. size and minimum contact frequency) for each ego network, and their average values. This allowed us to compare the ego network layers of Twitter ego networks with the results found in Facebook and in offline social networks.

The distribution of the optimal number of clusters of Twitter ego networks, obtained by iterating *k*-means with different values of *k* and by selecting the optimal clustering configuration for each ego network according to the AIC, is shown in Figure 4.4. Although the distribution is qualitatively similar to the distribution found in Facebook, it shows a slightly heavier tail.

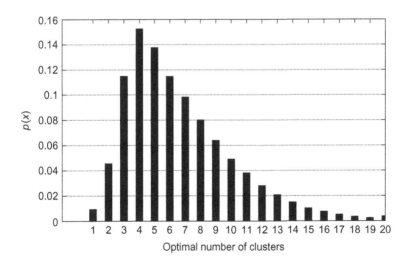

*Figure 4.4 Optimal number of clusters found by k-means with AIC on the ego networks of the Twitter dataset.*

This means that, compared to Facebook, the optimal number of clusters in Twitter ego networks has a higher variation. Nevertheless, the distribution clearly shows a peak between 4 and 5. The average value for the distribution is equal to 6.60, and the median is 5. The average silhouette value for the best configurations associated with the optimal number of clusters for each ego network is 0.674. This value is in accordance with the results obtained for Facebook ego networks, and indicates that the data are appropriately clustered, and the clusters in the Twitter ego networks are not fictitious. Since, unlike the case for the Facebook data, it is not possible to identify clearly a single value that is representative for all ego networks, we decided to apply the cluster analysis with fixed number of clusters using both 4 and 5 clusters, and then compare and discuss the results in terms of layer properties. The results, related to the configurations obtained with 4 and 5 clusters, are reported in Table 4.2. To test the validity of the results and to control for noisy data, we also calculated the size of the layers with DBSCAN. The results are reported in Table 4.3.

From the results in Table 4.2, the configuration for the Twitter data that best matches the properties of offline ego networks is the one involving five

**Table 4.2 Properties of Ego Network Layers in Twitter**

| Layer | 0 | 1 | 2 | 3 | 4 |
|---|---|---|---|---|---|
| Offline networks | | | | | |
| Size | ? | 5 | 15 | 50 | 150 |
| Contact freq. | ? | 48 | 12 | 2 | 1 |
| Twitter $k=4$ | | | | | |
| Size ($k$-means) | $1.87 \pm 0.03$ | $6.54 \pm 0.09$ | $21.09 \pm 0.27$ | – | $88.31 \pm 0.87$ |
| Contact freq. | $259.53 \pm 4.04$ | $93.03 \pm 1.31$ | $26.92 \pm 0.38$ | – | $2.54 \pm 0.02$ |
| Twitter $k=5$ | | | | | |
| Size ($k$-means) | $1.55 \pm 0.02$ | $4.52 \pm 0.06$ | $11.17 \pm 0.15$ | $28.28 \pm 0.32$ | $88.31 \pm 0.87$ |
| Contact freq. | $276.63 \pm 4.06$ | $113.12 \pm 1.49$ | $49.63 \pm 0.66$ | $16.89 \pm 0.21$ | $2.54 \pm 0.02$ |

**Table 4.3 Size of Ego Network Layers Found by DBSCAN**

| Layer | 0 | 1 | 2 | 3 | 4 |
|---|---|---|---|---|---|
| $k=4$ | | | | | |
| Size (DBSCAN) | $2.79 \pm 0.03$ | $6.86 \pm 0.11$ | $14.24 \pm 0.21$ | – | $77.72 \pm 1.15$ |
| $k=5$ | | | | | |
| Size (DBSCAN) | $2.59 \pm 0.03$ | $5.99 \pm 0.07$ | $10.71 \pm 0.13$ | $19.51 \pm 0.28$ | $85.35 \pm 1.15$ |

clusters. In particular, for this configuration, the size of the layers (both for $k$-means and DBSCAN) is very similar to that of offline layers. The values found in Twitter by DBSCAN are consistent with the results of $k$-means, indicating that the latter is effectively able to identify the correct clustering configuration for the ego networks.

### 4.3.3 Comparison Between Facebook and Twitter

The properties of Twitter ego networks are directly comparable to those found in Facebook and in offline environments. This indicates that the hierarchical structure of concentric layers of alters around the ego is consistent amongst different social environments, and is not influenced by the use of a particular communication medium. In addition, we also found in the Twitter dataset an inner circle of intimates consisting of $\sim$1.5 members who are contacted particularly frequently by the ego. This indicates that this circle is not an artefact of the particular properties of the Facebook datasets we analysed, but, instead, can be considered a characteristic property of ego networks, at least in the online environments we analysed. As with the Facebook ego networks, the outermost layer is smaller than the one in offline networks. This could be an effect of the measure used to estimate tie strength. In fact, the intimacy and the bi-directionality represented by a single reply in Twitter could be inappropriate for capturing weak social relationships, which could instead be maintained with other forms of communications (e.g. unidirectional communication through mentions).

The minimum contact frequency of the layers found in Twitter is higher than the one of layers in offline ego networks. This could be explained by the fact that tweets are very short messages (i.e. up to 140 characters only), and the emotional investment of a tweet is likely to be lower than an interaction in Facebook or face-to-face. In addition, several tweets could be part of a single interaction, with a thread of discussion between users, similar to what happens to SMS. Although the Twitter contact rates are, generally, somewhat higher than those for both the Facebook and face-to-face datasets (perhaps reflecting a lower time and emotional investment). Nonetheless, they are broadly similar, being only about twice the frequency of the latter, and in similar ratios across the layers.

From the combined analysis of Facebook and Twitter ego networks, we observe structural properties in OSNs that are qualitatively similar to those of offline social networks. This is a clear evidence of the presence of the cognitive and time constraints identified by the social brain hypothesis not only in offline environments, but also in OSNs. Nonetheless, the richness of OSN data allowed us to identify an additional element, the inner circle of ~1.5 alters, that has not previously been noted in offline data.

## 4.4 CHAPTER SUMMARY AND DISCUSSION

In this chapter, we presented an analysis aimed at characterising the properties of Twitter ego networks. We described the large-scale dataset we downloaded from Twitter, and we showed how we extracted the ego networks relevant for the analysis. As a first step, we considered the ego networks as static entities, and we studied the properties of their hierarchical structure in terms of layers by looking at the entire history of communications involving their social relationships. The most notable findings presented in the chapter are as follows.

### Dataset for the Analysis of Twitter Ego Networks

The dataset we obtained from Twitter contains the whole history of tweets of the users we sampled. This allowed us to reconstruct complete ego networks, and to obtain accurate results about their hierarchical structure. Moreover, the dataset contains records of communication which cover several years of social interactions of the users, up to about 7 years for the oldest Twitter accounts we downloaded. Usually, the datasets in the literature used for the analysis of evolutionary aspects of social networks cover only several months of communication. Our dataset allowed us to obtain significant results not only about the (static) structural properties of Twitter ego networks but also their dynamic properties over time. In the next chapter, we exploit this to explore some of the evolutionary aspects of these networks.

### The Structure of Ego Networks in Twitter

Twitter users are not only people that use the platform for socialising with others but also companies, public figures and other types of accounts not representative of the social behaviour of humans at large. For this reason, we created a method to automatically extract 'socially relevant users' from the dataset based on supervised learning. A first analysis on the average tie strength of the relevant ego networks as a function of their size revealed the presence of cognitive and time constraints that limit the number of active social relationships that each user can maintain at a certain level of intimacy. A deeper analysis of Twitter ego networks revealed that the size of their layers is very similar to the ones found in Facebook and in offline environments. However, the contact frequency of the layers in Twitter is more than twice those for Facebook and offline. This could be due to the nature of Twitter communication, which is characterised by short but frequent messages. As in Facebook, we found an internal inner layer of one or two 'intimates', with very high contact frequencies with the ego. That we find this layer appears in two of the most important, yet very different, OSNs greatly strengthens the claim for its existence as a real layer in people's natural networks. The most external layer (the active network) appears to be smaller in Twitter than offline. This could be explained by the fact that in Twitter, as in Facebook, people tend to develop their personal social network starting from friends they already know in real life, and the dataset might contain ego networks that are still not completely developed in their outermost layers.

# CHAPTER 5

# Evolutionary Dynamics in Twitter Ego Networks

## 5.1 INTRODUCTION

In this chapter, we present an analysis on the dynamics of the properties of social relationships and ego networks in Twitter. We performed this analysis on the same dataset described in Chapter 4. Thanks to the detailed temporal information and the large quantity of data contained in the dataset, we have been able to create a time series for each ego network, and then study how the size and the composition of each ego network layer, as well as the properties of single social relationships, evolved over time. This extends and integrates the analysis on the properties of the layers of ego networks presented in the previous chapter, by providing a detailed characterisation of the dynamic properties of ego networks in online environments. The chapter is structured as follows. In Section 5.2, we summarise the work in the literature on the evolution of social networks, and we motivate the need of our work. Then, in Section 5.3, we describe the methodology we used in our analysis. Next, in Section 5.4, we present the results of the analysis, divided into separate sections for each property we consider.

## 5.2 EVOLUTIONARY PROPERTIES OF SOCIAL NETWORK GRAPHS

In the last few years, a lot of work has been devoted to understanding the mechanisms controlling the evolution of social networks. From a macro-level perspective, being able to predict how a social network will evolve is clearly important in a number of different fields. For example, if a company running a social networking service could predict in advance whether the number of their users will grow or decline in the future, they could adopt the right marketing strategies. On the other hand, understanding the evolution of social networks at the microscopic level could reveal how egocentric social structures are formed and maintained over time. Whilst most of the work in the literature is focussed on evolutionary analyses of social networks at the macroscopic level, our knowledge about evolutionary aspects at the microscopic level is still limited. In this section, we give a brief overview of the findings in the literature concerning micro-level properties of online social networks (OSNs). For a complete overview of the evolutionary aspects of network graphs, we refer the reader to [94]. Note that, although some evolutionary properties of ego networks in OSNs are already known, there are no detailed results about the evolution of Twitter ego networks.

Zhao et al. [95] analysed the evolution of a large-scale Chinese social network over a 2-year period from the creation of the first user accounts to a time when it included 19 million users and 199 million edges. They analysed the network dynamics at three different levels: (i) individual user, (ii) community and (iii) network. The results at the individual level reveal that users add social relationships in their ego network at a higher rate when they join the platform, and then they tend to maintain a constant rate over time. New communities are constantly created, but shortly after their creation they can merge into other larger communities. Lastly, the data analysed by these authors captured the uncommon event of the merging of two OSNs, which became a unique service at a certain time. The event impacted on the behaviour of the users and their properties, but after a while the network returned to exhibit properties similar to those observed before the merge. This indicates an invariance of the properties of the network. This invariance is also visible in the general statistics of the network graph, which remain the same despite nodes and edges in the network being constantly created whilst the activity on edges is not constant, but bursty.

Miritello et al. [96] performed a detailed analysis on a large-scale dataset containing information about phone calls of a single operator, focussing on the activation/deactivation patterns in the interaction graph at the level of ego networks. The authors introduced the notion of *communication capacity* and *communication activity* of the ego, where the former is a measure of the number of relationships that a user manages instantaneously, whereas the latter measures the total number of social relationships that the user creates, and the rates at which he or she does so. The study revealed that, despite the bursty nature of the activity on social links, the communication capacity of the users is limited, and remains constant over time. On the other hand, the communication activity is higher at the beginning of the user's lifetime (i.e. new links are created mostly when users first begin using the service), but eventually reaches a constant rate. The communication capacity is proportional to the communication activity, in the sense that users that add links more rapidly usually maintain more active relationships instantly.

This is in accordance with the preferential attachment rule. Interestingly, the data also reveal a preferential detachment rule, whereby users with higher communication capacity deactivate a higher number of links. Users also tend to maintain a core set of social relationships which they maintain in their ego network. In fact, on average, 75% of the relationships are actively maintained over a period of 7 months. Nevertheless, this behaviour is inhomogeneous, and for some users, called *social keepers*, the core network reaches 90% of the relationships, whilst for those called *social explorers* it is 52%.

Another work presented by Viswanath et al. [85] analysed the evolution of the interaction graph in Facebook at both micro- and macro-level. The results indicate that, in accordance with the already presented studies, links in the ego networks are activated and deactivated rapidly, and their strength generally decreases over time soon after their creation. At the macroscopic level, even though the social graph is in constant expansion, the general properties of the interaction graph (e.g. clustering coefficient, diameter) remain invariant to the continuous activation and deactivation of links.

The results found in the literature indicate the presence of a process whereby social links are continuously activated and deactivated, but the communication capacity of the users remains constant. The general behaviour of the users seems to be to establish more links soon after they join the network, and then to maintain a stable communication activity over time. These findings indicate that the properties of social networks at the microscopic level are influenced by the presence of cognitive constraints in human social behaviour. At a higher-level perspective, link creation in social networks is controlled by the presence of influential nodes, which generally attract more links than others, following the preferential attachment rule. Communities are formed and maintained by charismatic users that serve as local influencers to develop the more peripheral parts of the network.

In these aspects, the patterns we observe in the online world seem to mirror what happens in the offline world. In a study of mobile phone use by university students, Saramäki et al. [97] found that despite up to 40% turnover in network membership over an 18-month period, the way in which egos distributed their social effort (irrespective of whether this was indexed by the frequency of phone calls, the frequency of texts or self-ratings of emotional closeness) remained constant over time. They interpreted this as suggesting that each person has a kind of social 'signature' (or style) that dictates how they invest cognitive effort in the alters in their network, and that this remains constant, even if the identity of the individuals occupying the different slots changes.

In sum, it seems that the global properties of the network are invariant to the constant activation and deactivation of social links. This could reflect the combined effect of the constrained nature of human social behaviour and the presence of global rules controlling the creation of new links, involving preferential attachment and the organisation into communities.

Although these results can be explained by the presence of cognitive constraints of the human brain in the formation of social structures in the network, there are still some points that need further investigation. Specifically, it is not clear how the layers of the ego networks evolve over time, and there is the lack of a direct comparison between the dynamic properties of offline social networks and OSNs. In the following sections, we present our contribution to the field, which is aimed at bridging this gap by providing, first, an analysis of the dynamics of the layers of Twitter ego networks and then, second, a comparison with the results found offline (i.e. from the analysis of phone call records presented in [96, 98]).

## 5.3 METHODOLOGY FOR THE ANALYSIS OF THE DYNAMICS OF TWITTER EGO NETWORKS

We studied the time series of directed tweets generated by each ego in our Twitter dataset to understand how the strength of social relationships evolves over time, as well as the dynamics of the structural properties of complete ego networks. Moreover, we studied undirected tweets to understand how users modify their usage of Twitter in terms of broadcast communication over time.

For some performance indices (i.e. communication capacity and activity), we counted the number of new alters contacted by the ego each day within its active lifespan. Here, in order to analyse the dynamics of the ego network structure we proceeded in a slightly different way: we sliced the tweets time series taking a temporal window of 1 year, then assessed the size and the composition of the ego network in that window. For each ego network, we moved the temporal window of 1 year from the first interaction by the ego to the last one, with a step of 1 day, and we calculated the size of each ego network layer in each successive 1 year window. Since the analysis is based on temporal windows of 1 year, we further filtered the dataset, eliminating all the profiles created less than 1 year before the time of their download. The dataset, after this filtering, consists of 644,014 accounts.

By taking temporal windows of 1 year we were able to capture all the active contacts maintained by each ego and their evolution over time, according to the definition of active network in the ego network model (i.e. everyone contacted at least once a year [63]). In this way, we were also able to identify relationships that the users abandoned over time. Note that we do not use the notion of 'unfollowing' (i.e. the explicit request of a user to remove a person from her friends) to identify abandoned relationships, since unfollowing is an extreme action that does not capture the more gradual decline of a natural social link, but rather identifies a sudden breach in the relationship that typically occur in response to unusually negative and typically rare events.

In contrast to the analysis presented in Section 4.3, here we define the layers of the ego networks according to fixed values of contact frequency of the relationships. In this way, we simplify the analysis by avoiding the need to apply clustering algorithms on each temporal window of each ego network. Since we move the temporal window with a step of 1 day, the number of windows we would have to analyse with cluster analysis is equal to the number of days of the active lifespan of the users, and is far too large for any sensible analysis. Thus, following the results found in offline social networks, we defined the sympathy group as the set of alters contacted at least once a month (i.e. contacted at least 12.17 times in 1 year), the support clique as the set of alters contacted once a week (i.e. contacted more than 52.14 times in 1 year) and the active network as the set of alters contacted at least once a year. We did not analyse the affinity group since we lack precise information about the contact frequency of this layer in offline ego networks. Note that these assumptions allowed us to significantly simplify the analysis, but, at the same time, to obtain a detailed view of the dynamic evolution of Twitter ego networks over time.

To be able to analyse the average behaviour of all ego networks, we shifted the first communication of each ego network (the time when ego started to actively communicate), so that they start at the same point in time, specifically at the origin of the coordinate system of each figure reported in the following. We did not normalise the duration of the relationships to have a more accurate view of the temporal dynamics, and to be able to compare the properties of relationships day after day. In the figures depicted in the following, we report the average values as the curve in bold and the corresponding 95% confidence interval as a lighter coloured area around the curve (barely visible, most of the time).

To analyse the behaviour of different users in Twitter in greater depth, we divided them into three categories based on the duration of their active lifespan, and we studied the differences in terms of social behaviour between these classes. To do so, we take the maximum lifespan in the dataset and we divide it into three equal parts, obtaining three groups of 802 days of duration each. We created exactly three categories since this choice represents a good trade-off between the accuracy of the results and their statistical significance. In fact, adding more categories would have decreased the number of users in each group, leading to low significance. We defined the following classes of users: (i) occasional users (lifespan $\leq$ 802 days), (ii) regular users (802 $<$ lifespan $\leq$ 1604 days) and (iii) aficionados (lifespan $>$ 1604 days). The dataset is composed of 63.23% of occasional users, 35.22% of regular users and 1.55% of aficionados. Note that we still have around 10,000 aficionados in our dataset, which makes the analysis of this class significant.

## 5.4 DYNAMICS OF TWITTER EGO NETWORKS
### 5.4.1 Evolution of Personal Social Relationships
To understand the dynamics of single social relationships, we analysed the evolution of the recency of contact (i.e. time since last contact) between users. To do so, we measured the time elapsed between consecutive messages within each relationship. We averaged the results within each ego network, and then for all the ego networks. While this clearly mixes the properties of different type of social relationships for a particular ego network, it provides a unique index that allows us to compare the ego networks of different classes of users.

To better characterise the properties of single social relationships in each class of users, we divided them according to their duration into 'short' relationships (i.e. with duration lower than the half of the maximum duration in the class of users) and 'long' relationships (i.e. with duration greater than the half of the maximum duration).

Figure 5.1 shows the number of days since last contact between people involved in each social relationship (on the $y$-axis) as a function of the time

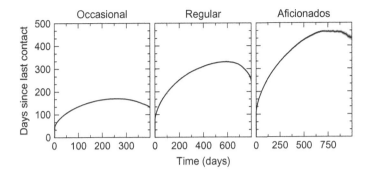

*Figure 5.1 Days since last contact evolution over time for social relationships with short duration.*

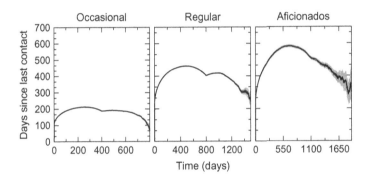

*Figure 5.2 Days since last contact evolution over time for social relationships with long duration.*

since the beginning of the relationship ($x$-axis), for short social relationships. Similarly, Figure 5.2 shows the evolution of the number of days since last contact for long relationships. From the figures, we can see that all the distributions show a 'bow' shaped curve. This particular shape tells us that, on the one hand, social relationships have an initial phase in which they have a shorter time since last contact (i.e. higher frequency of contact) followed by a gradual increment. On the other hand, since some social relationships are deactivated as time passes, the remaining social relationships, being the most long-lived, are those showing higher frequency of contact. This explains the gradual decay in the right most part of the graphs.

It is worth noting that there is a significant variation in the values of time since last contact in the different categories of users, with occasional users having lower values compared to the other classes. The results are in accordance with previous findings on different OSNs. Specifically, the activity on social links shows an initial boost, and then a gradual decay.

## 5.4.2 Users Leaving Twitter

We say that a user has left Twitter if her active lifespan is followed by a period of at least 6 months of inactivity (i.e. all social links are inactive for more than 6 months). In the dataset, the average active lifespan of users that left Twitter is 73.21 days, indicating that most of them are occasional users. In fact, out of a total of 159,069 accounts that left Twitter (i.e. 24.7% of our dataset), 88.27% are occasional users, whilst only 11.6% are regular users and 0.13% are aficionados. These results indicate that many of the users in the dataset interacted with other users only in the early phase of a relationship, but then they stopped their involvement. These users are compatible with the definition of *passive* users given in [35].

## 5.4.3 Undirected Communications

We studied how the intensity of undirected tweets (i.e. plain text tweets, tweets with hashtags and tweets with URLs) change over time for the different categories of users. The results for plain text tweets are shown in Figure 5.3, whereas the results for tweets containing hashtags and for tweets containing URLs are shown in Figures 5.4 and 5.5, respectively. Occasional users significantly decrease the amount of undirected tweets they send over time – apart from tweets with URLs, although these are very limited in number. This category of users shows an initial boost of activity followed by a gradual decrease, as already found for directed communications on single social links. Regular users show a much more stable trend for the

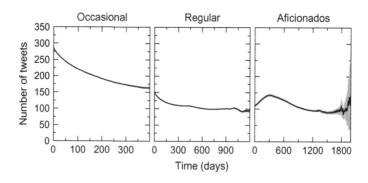

*Figure 5.3 Undirected communications – plain text tweets.*

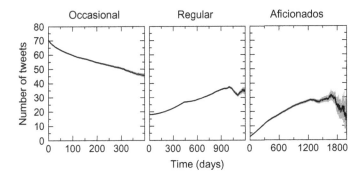

*Figure 5.4 Undirected communications – tweets with hashtags.*

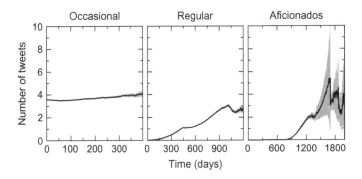

*Figure 5.5 Undirected communications – tweets with URLs.*

number of plain text tweets, with a value asymptotically converging towards ~100 tweets sent in each 1-year window. Yet, the number of undirected tweets is noticeably lower than for the previous category, even though it is increasing over time. This indicates that regular users are less affected by an initial boost, and instead they typically have a slow start. Aficionados show a similar pattern, apart from plain text tweets, which show a peak in the first 2 years of their active lifespan. This peak could be due to an initial enthusiasm in the platform at a global level, since this category contains some of the oldest profiles in Twitter. After this initial phase, the number of plain text tweets asymptotically converges to a value similar to that for the other classes.

These results tell us that whilst some users cease their activity on Twitter after a short period of time, the users which continue to use the platform show a stable level of activity, rejecting the hypothesis of a convergence towards a constant decline of the activity in the network [99]. This is in contrast with the results of [27], where the authors found that, in Facebook, users are more active when they join the network, decreasing their use rate over time. Our analysis reveals that this behaviour is true only for occasional users and that there is a non-negligible amount of long-term users contributing to the survival of Twitter.

### 5.4.4 Communication Activity

We depict the evolution of communication activity of the users, both in terms of cumulative number of social links added up to a certain time (Figure 5.6), and the instantaneous number of new links (Figure 5.7). The values are averaged for all the sampled users. From the graphs in the figures, it is clear that, after a first phase in which ego contacts new people at a high rate, there is a rapid convergence to a constant in the number of new alters contacted. The value of this constant is higher for occasional users than for the other classes. The mean over time is 0.222, 0.125 and 0.112 for the three classes, respectively. Note that, even though the slopes of the three curves related to the 'daily' activity pattern seem to be similar, the values on the $x$ scale are not. This indicates that occasional users have more dynamic ego networks, with a higher number of new social links added over time compared to the other categories. We can notice that the total number of different people contacted by egos over time is, on average about 200 and it is constantly growing, with little variation between the different classes, even though the duration of the ego networks varies considerably between classes. These results are in accordance with the findings in the literature, where users have been found to be more active in creating new social links shortly after joining a network. This could be explained by the tendency

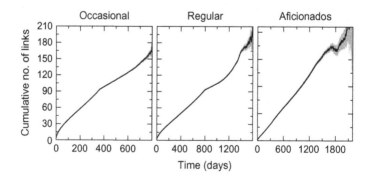

*Figure 5.6 Communication activity – average cumulative number of links established by egos over time.*

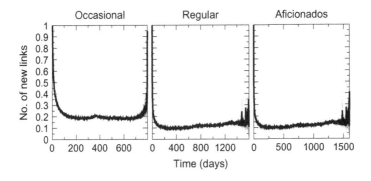

*Figure 5.7 Communication activity – average number of new links established by egos each day.*

of users to rapidly recreate their offline social environment when they join Twitter, by adding contacts they know in the offline world. After this phase, new links are created at a lower rate, and the users eventually approach a constant number of edges created per time unit once most offline friends have been found and linked.

To understand how the constant addition of new contacts in the ego networks impacts on the communication level with the set of existing alters, we studied the evolution of the size of the set of alters actively maintained over time. We also report an analysis of the percentage of turnover (i.e. the degree of variation in the set of alters actively contacted) for the different layers in the ego networks.

## 5.4.5 Communication Capacity and Dynamics of Ego Network Layers

The evolution over time of the size of the ego network layers are shown in Figure 5.8 for the support clique, Figure 5.9 for the sympathy group and Figure 5.10 for the active network. Note that, in the figures, the value of the $x$-axis represents the starting point of each snapshot. Thus, the maximum value of the axis is equal to the maximum lifespan of the ego networks in the relevant class, minus the duration of the snapshot (1 year). The depicted sizes represent the communication capacity of users, since they indicate the number of social relationships actively maintained over time, in each of the three layers. The figures indicate that, even though the communication activity of the users increases over time at a constant rate, the communication capacity does not. In fact, as far as occasional users are concerned, the size of all the layers significantly decreases over time. Specifically, the active network has a total decrease of 30.7%, the sympathy

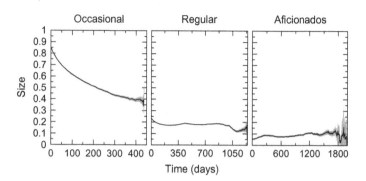

*Figure 5.8 Communication capacity – support clique.*

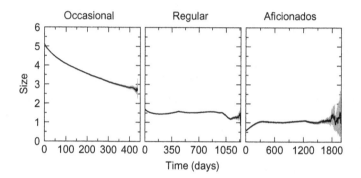

*Figure 5.9 Communication capacity – sympathy group.*

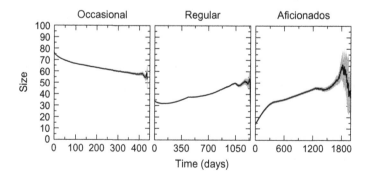

*Figure 5.10 Communication capacity – active network.*

group of 45.9% and the support clique of 53.2%. Regular users behave differently, with a considerable increase in the active network size (31.2% in almost 4 years), but with a decrease in the other layers (32.2% for the sympathy group and 30.4% for the support clique). It is worth noting that occasional users, compared to regular users, show a higher communication activity and larger sizes in all the layers at the beginning of their lifespan, but eventually approach sizes comparable to those of regular users. Aficionados show a considerable growth in size in all the ego network layers, even though their communication activity is lower than for the other categories.

These results highlight how the behaviour of users in Twitter can differ and indicate that occasional users have an initial boost of activity followed by a decrease or a sudden abandonment of the platform. Regular users and aficionados have a slower start, but they eventually increase the size of their active network over time. Aficionados even increase the size of their inner layers, indicating an investment in strong social relationships, maybe due to the longevity of such relationships, which are constantly reinforced through Twitter.

From the analysis of communication activity and capacity for the three classes of users, we can qualitatively say that the rate at which egos contact new users is negatively correlated with the growth rate of their ego network layers, indicating that users who spend a lot of their time adding new people into their networks (occasional users) do not have sufficient resources to maintain all these relationships over time; as a result, their layers inevitably decrease in size. This is in accordance with the idea that our social capacity is limited by cognitive constraints and going beyond our limits could even result in the breakup of our social networks [61].

### 5.4.6 Ego Network Turnover

After examining the evolution of ego networks and personal social relationships over time, we measured the stability of ego networks, and assessed the proportion of alters that users maintain in their networks over time. We estimated this proportion by comparing consecutive – but separated – 1-year snapshots and calculating their average Jaccard coefficient, then averaging the results for all the ego networks. The Jaccard coefficient is a measure of the percentage of overlap between sets defined as:

$$J(W_1, W_2) = \frac{|W_1 \cap W_2|}{|W_1 \cup W_2|} \qquad (5.1)$$

where $W_1$ and $W_2$ are two sets, in our case the 1-year windows of the ego networks. The Jaccard coefficient can be a value between 0 and 1, with 0 indicating no overlap and 1 complete overlap between the sets. We calculated the Jaccard coefficient for the different layers in the ego networks. This allowed us to determine the 'turnover' that takes place in the ego networks. Thus, we can discover whether people maintain a stable network of contacts in Twitter or prefer to vary their social relationships over time, and so allows us to define two distinct classes of users: (i) users with structured ego networks, showing ego networks whose composition and turnover is similar to those found in other more traditional social networks and (ii) people without structured ego networks, showing higher turnover.

To perform this analysis, we further reduced the number of ego networks in the dataset, since we needed at least 2 years of active lifespan to calculate the Jaccard coefficient between two different non-overlapping 1-year windows. Thus, we selected 190,249 ego networks with active lifespan greater than 2 years.

The average Jaccard coefficients for the different layers are reported in Table 5.1 under the label 'all ego networks'. The low values of Jaccard coefficient for all the layers indicate that the turnover is generally greater than 75%, with a maximum of 98.8% for the support clique of aficionados. This reveals that the average turnover in each layer is really high, especially when compared to the results found in offline environments, where the turnover is more typically in the region of ~40% [97]. This turnover can be explained as the combined effect of the limited communication capacity of users, and their constant communication activity. In fact, as users constantly

| Table 5.1 Average Jaccard Coefficient of Different Network Layers | | | |
|---|---|---|---|
| Layer | Occasional | Regular | Aficionados |
| *All ego networks* | | | |
| Active net | 0.124 | 0.098 | 0.103 |
| Sympathy gr. | 0.122 | 0.075 | 0.072 |
| Support cl. | 0.057 | 0.024 | 0.012 |
| *Structured ego networks* | | | |
| Active net | 0.191 | 0.190 | 0.193 |
| Sympathy gr. | 0.287 | 0.309 | 0.362 |
| Support cl. | 0.346 | 0.395 | 0.488 |

add new contacts in their networks, they must deactivate some of the existing relationships to make room for the new ones. Interestingly, the turnover in the inner layers is higher than the turnover in the active network. This result contrasts the findings on other social communication media, for example, the results on phone call records analysed in [96, 97], where the authors found that for the top 20 ranking alters in ego networks – formed of social links weighted with the number of calls between people in a fixed time period – the turnover is much lower than for the rest of the ego network. It is also worth noting that occasional users show higher stability compared to the other classes. This result could be explained by the fact that the longer the lifespan, the higher is the probability that the social relationships in the ego network change due to turnover.

The low values of Jaccard coefficient in the inner layers (i.e. 0.057 for occasional users, 0.024 for regular users and 0.012 for aficionados) could be influenced by the presence of small support cliques and sympathy groups, which for many egos do not even exist. For this reason, we decided to calculate the Jaccard coefficients considering only users that always maintain a structured ego network, or, in other words, that show a non-empty support clique in all the sampled 1-year windows. The number of ego networks that show a turnover pattern similar to those found in other social environments is 10,307, only 5.42% of the egos in our sample for this analysis. This is another strong indication that human behaviour in Twitter differs significantly from other social environments that involve more traditional and dyadic communications. The results are reported in Table 5.1 under the heading 'structured ego network'. In this case, the values on the Jaccard coefficient for the different layers are higher than in the previous case and are compatible with the findings in [96, 97]. The values of the percentage turnover in the active networks are similar for all the different categories and are about 81% (Jaccard coefficient $\sim$0.19). For the other layers, the sympathy groups show a percentage turnover between 71.3% and 63.8%, whereas for support cliques it is between 65.4% and 51.2%. These results indicate behaviour similar to other social networks, where the inner layers contain stronger relationships that we would expect to be less affected by the turnover in the network. Nevertheless, as already found in [97], the inner layers are still affected by turnover to some extent. Remarkably, in structured ego networks, the categories of users with longer lifespan have higher values of Jaccard coefficient, especially for the inner layers. This tells us that users that maintain structured ego networks tend to invest their time and effort in reinforcing their existing close relationships over time, instead of devoting time to weak relationships. Note that this is in accordance with the analysis of the evolution of the sizes of the layers over time for aficionados, reported earlier.

We have also analysed the properties of the 10,307 'structured' ego networks by calculating their active lifespan, and the communication activity and capacity for their ego layers (using the same technique described in Section 5.4.5 above). The results of the communication activity are shown in Figure 5.11, whilst the results of the communication capacity are depicted in Figure 5.12. The active lifespan of these ego networks ranges between 730 and 1749 days. These are the minimum and maximum active lifetimes of ego networks in our dataset that always presented a non-empty support clique. This definition allowed us to isolate users with behaviour similar to that found in 'offline' environments, where the support clique is maintained over time by the majority of people as the most important part of their network.

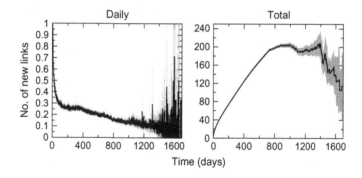

*Figure 5.11 Communication activity of structured ego networks.*

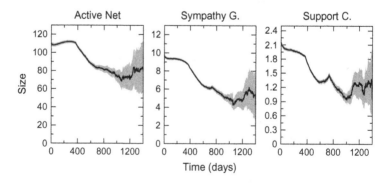

*Figure 5.12 Communication capacity of structured ego networks.*

Interestingly, the layers of the structured ego networks are larger than the average, resembling the layers found in Chapter 4 (Section 4.3). Remarkably, all the layers decrease in size as time passes and so does the number of new alters contacted by ego. This could be explained by the presence of the initial boost of social activity of occasional users. Nevertheless, egos with longer lifespans prefer to consolidate their social relationships than adding new contacts, as indicated by the decrease in the graphs in Figure 5.11. This is in accordance with the results presented in the previous sections.

## 5.5 CHAPTER SUMMARY AND DISCUSSION

In this chapter, we studied the same ego networks from our Twitter dataset as we studied in Chapter 4, but here focussed on exploring their dynamic evolution. To this end, we analysed how the size and composition of each ego network layer changed over time. To do this, we took snapshots of all the social interactions in the ego networks of 1 year each, and then we analysed the dynamics of the ego networks from the moment the egos joined Twitter until the last day of communications we have been able to download.

Our analyses have shown that ego networks are not static, but instead evolve over time. The cumulative number of social relationships established by an ego over time (i.e. its communication activity) shows an initial burst when the ego joins the online platform, and then gradually converges to a constant value. This has been found in several other OSN environments, and is confirmed by our results in Twitter. When we look at the number of social relationships instantly maintained by the egos as active (i.e. its communication capacity), we find that this remains constant over time, probably as a direct consequence of the limited cognitive capacity of the human brain, and of the limited time people have for socialising. As far as single social relationships are concerned, their evolution typically starts from an initial burst of activity followed by a gradual decay. Whilst most of the relationships decline after a short period of time, some long-lasting relationships endure. These relationships are generally associated with high levels of contact frequency, and are thus the core relationships of the egos.

The turnover rate in Twitter ego networks is much higher than in offline ego networks, and social relationships in Twitter are created and forgotten at a higher rate. This difference in turnover rate can probably be attributed to the fact that offline networks typically consist of a mixture of family members and friends, whereas online, and especially in Twitter, networks are probably mainly only friends (see Chapter 2). In offline ego networks, about 50% of the alters are members of ego's extended family, at least in European samples, with priority often being given to family members [63]. Compared to friendships, family relationships are relatively robust to destabilising influences such as reduced frequencies of interaction [67].

This indicates that even though the structural properties of Twitter ego networks are similar to those found offline, the dynamism of these networks reveals some important differences between online and offline social environments. In many ways, social platforms like Twitter seem to be the perfect tool for maintaining social relationships within a society asking for fast and constant changes in one's social life in which there is an opportunity for high turnover of network members – in effect, for those who pursue a 'social butterfly' strategy. Nonetheless, there is a noticeable subset of Twitter users that seem to use this medium in a more 'conventional' way to keep social relationships alive. These users show more stable ego network structures, which always present several layers of differing intimacy much as we see in the offline world. This may simply reflect the wide natural diversity of personality function [100]. OSNs like Twitter may suit a particular personality types, but not necessarily suit others.

# CHAPTER 6

# Conclusion

## 6.1 INTRODUCTION

In this chapter, we discuss how the structural properties of ego networks found in online social networks (OSNs) can be exploited to extend existing analyses on social phenomena (e.g. models of information diffusion) and to create novel online communication services and applications, and we summarise the main findings presented in this book.

In Section 6.2, we discuss the impact of the structural properties of ego networks on information diffusion in social networks and we present some of the most recent information diffusion analyses that exploit these properties. Then, in Section 6.3, we consider how such properties could be exploited to improve online services and applications. Specifically, we present solutions based on the structural properties of ego networks for the creation of distributed OSNs (DOSNs), a new form of OSNs that provide users with a higher level of control and privacy than traditional platforms. In addition, we discuss how the results of generative models of social network graphs can be improved by using the results shown in this book. Finally, in Section 6.4, we conclude the book, with a brief summary of the main findings that we presented in the previous chapters.

## 6.2 EGO NETWORK STRUCTURE AND INFORMATION DIFFUSION

Social networks are a prominent tool for the diffusion of information in society. Therefore, modelling and predicting information diffusion through social networks is a hot research topic that has attracted a lot of interest in recent years, in particular after the advent of OSNs. Being able to predict (and possibly induce) large-scale information spread would clearly be important for a number of applications, including advertising and other marketing campaigns, as well as political campaigns. From the literature, it is known that tie strength has a direct impact on information diffusion. In fact, the amount of information exchanged between users is correlated with the strength of their social relationship [101]. Moreover, although there are many possible factors external to social relationships influencing the diffusion of information [102], a large portion of diffusion (estimated at over 50% [103]) maps onto social relationships between people, producing the so-called 'word-of-mouth' effect. This typically generates 'cascades' of information flowing through the network. Some existing models aim to reproduce these cascades by predicting how information will be diffused between pairs of nodes, according to the strength of their social relationship.

The simplest and most widely used models of information diffusion are the independent cascades (IC) and the linear threshold (LT) models. In the case of IC, newly activated nodes (i.e. nodes that receive information) try to activate their neighbours with a probability of diffusion defined by their social links. This procedure is iterated in discrete steps until no more nodes are activated. In case of LT, the inactive nodes are activated if the sum of the strengths on the social links of neighbours that have already been activated exceeds a certain threshold. Another class of information diffusion models tries to identify influential information spreaders by looking at the properties of the social network graph itself. The assumption underpinning these models is that nodes in core regions of the network are usually more active in the diffusion of information, and that information cascades starting from these nodes are often larger than diffusions starting from other nodes.

The results presented in this book on the structure of ego networks in OSNs are relevant to several aspects of information diffusion. Models for the prediction of tie strength could be used to improve the estimation of the probability of diffusion between nodes in a way that may be very relevant to information diffusion models such as the IC and the LT. Moreover, differences in the structural properties of ego networks (e.g. size, number of layers, tie strength distribution) could be useful for identifying influential information spreaders.

An example of information diffusion analysis that integrates concepts derived from the structural properties of ego networks is provided by the work presented in [104], which aimed at discovering the relation between the properties of ego networks, namely the size and the tie strength distribution, and the size and depth of information cascades generated by egos. This study simulated the formation of information cascades using the IC model. A cascade is started from each node in the network, and, at each step of the IC, information is propagated through social links according to a probability proportional to tie strength, calculated as the normalised contact frequency between users. In addition, an ageing factor was added to the model to penalise the diffusion of old messages. Once cascades happened, the authors of this study analysed the correlations between several possible indices of the ego network around each node (e.g. node degree, node weighted degree, PageRank, Burt's constraint), with or without considering tie strength, and (i) the number of nodes activated by the diffusion cascades that start from the same nodes and (ii) the depth of the resulting cascades. The results indicate that when tie strength is taken into account, all the considered indices (and their weighted versions) are highly correlated with the size and the depth of the cascades. The index that provides the best correlation is the weighted degree, with a correlation coefficient higher than 0.7 for both the size and depth of cascades. When tie strength is not considered, the correlation is significantly lower. The correlation for the unweighted degree is, on average, around 0.2 for both the size and the depth of cascades. These results indicate that influential spreaders can be effectively identified by looking at the properties of their ego networks, and at the weighted node degree in particular, but only when detailed information about the strength of their social relationships is available. Specifically, influential spreaders are users with high levels of activity with others (identified by their weighted degree), and with a central position in their ego networks (identified by Burt's constraint and other ego centrality measures). Notably, the size of ego networks is not predictive of the influence of the node in the diffusion process.

The work presented in [105] represents an additional example of how to extend existing information diffusion models using the knowledge about the structural properties of ego networks. The work assesses the impact of limiting the ego network of each user, by eliminating social relationships outside certain layers, on the capacity of the whole network to diffuse information. The analysis is performed on a large-scale OSN dataset, generating four sub-graphs containing, respectively, the support cliques of the ego networks in the dataset, their sympathy groups, their affinity groups and their active networks. The analysis of these sub-graphs indicate that after limiting all the ego networks to their active network layer, and discarding social relationships outside it, the resulting network is still well-connected, and the giant component of the sub-graph contains 96.6% of the nodes in the giant component of the original network. This means that the network is still able to support the diffusion of information to a large portion of its nodes. On the other hand, the giant components of the other sub-graphs cover only 29.7% of the original network for the sub-graph limited to the affinity group, 19.1% for the sympathy group and 2.8% for the support clique. These results indicate that the capacity of the network to diffuse information could be severely limited if only the inner layers of the ego networks are used for the diffusion process. This is in accordance with the theory of 'the strength of weak ties' by Mark Granovetter [45], whereby information reaches distant and otherwise disconnected parts of social networks by following bridges, which, as we have seen in Chapter 2, are weak ties. Thus, eliminating weak ties could lead to the formation of isolated parts of the network, limiting information diffusion. Nonetheless, the results indicate that weak ties outside the active network of the users are useless for information diffusion since their level of activity is too low, and information rarely flows through them. At least in offline networks, the alters in inner layers are often densely interconnected, but those in the outer layers are not (except in the case of the family sub-network) [62]. In such cases, the outer layers may resemble more of a 'hub-and-spokes' model (in which individual non-family alters are linked directly to ego), whilst the inner layers may be completely connected. For this reason, removing weak links in the outer layers may have only a limited effect on the network's normal capacity to diffuse information. It is worth noting that this study did not assess the impact of the removal of inner circles only (i.e. by keeping just the outer layers) on the information diffusion capacity of the network. In practice, of course, this would be extremely difficult to engineer in the real world, and hence very rare (except, perhaps, in times of catastrophic natural disasters such as floods or war).

In [105], the authors also proposed a possible method for increasing the number of nodes in the giant component of the analysed sub-graphs, by re-inserting in the sub-graphs a single relationship for each user outside the relevant ego network layer. Several possible strategies for the selection of these social relationships have been tested, including the selection of the relationship with highest (or lowest) contact frequency, and according to a probability proportional (or inversely proportional) to the contact frequency, as well as a random strategy. The best strategy, in terms of effect on the size of the giant components, is the re-insertion in the sub-graph of social links according to a probability proportional to its level of contact frequency (but under the threshold of the respective ego network layer) for each user (i.e. a very weak 'weak link'). This strategy selects strong ties most of the time, but sometimes also weak ties with a probability greater than 0, guaranteeing the presence of bridges in the network, and thus re-including many otherwise disconnected components in the giant components of the sub-graphs. The strategy increases the proportion of the sub-graph that consists of active networks to 99.4% of the original network, to 72.6% for affinity groups, 66.1% for sympathy groups and 45.3% for support cliques. In other words, this strategy significantly increases the size of the giant components, thereby significantly improving the network's capacity to diffuse information, potentially supporting larger information cascades than sub-graphs without re-insertion.

## 6.3 RESEARCH DIRECTIONS

In this final section, we present some ongoing work on OSNs that may benefit from the results presented in this book. Specifically, we present solutions for distributed OSNs, a decentralised and privacy-aware alternative to traditional social media, and for models for the generation of synthetic social network graphs based on the structural properties of ego networks.

**Distributed Online Social Networks**

Online social networks store and aggregate all the data generated by their users into central servers. These data are usually the property of service providers, and are only partially accessible by other individuals. This results in users having only a limited level of control over their personal data, as well as limited openness for the service as a whole. As a possible solution to overcome these limitations, DOSNs have been recently proposed. Examples include Diaspora [106], Peerson [107] and Safebook [108]. DOSNs implement OSN functionalities, but in a completely decentralised way. User-generated content remains on the personal devices of the users or is replicated on a limited number of additional nodes, with links to these nodes governed by openness and trust. For a more complete discussion on DOSNs, we refer the reader to the work by Paul et al. [109].

In DOSNs, content exchange is directly managed between users' devices, and is usually performed through peer-to-peer networking, without the need for central servers. One of the main issues with DOSNs is data availability. Since content is maintained on users' devices, which could suffer from periodic disconnections from the network or from switch-offs, requests could fail, thus limiting the usability of the system. To improve data availability, replication schemes are usually adopted.

Several replication strategies have been proposed in the literature. For example, Han et al. [110] presented a social selection scheme that identifies hosts for replicas as the neighbours of a node potentially able to serve the highest number of other neighbours in the ego network. Similarly, Xia et al. [111] propose an algorithm for efficient replica allocation that selects the smallest set of neighbours of a node which serve the largest number of other neighbours, based on the topology of the network formed of social relationships existing between users. Although these solutions provide valid replication schemes from a technological point of view, they do not consider the trust level between users.

It is important to note that, in DOSNs, users would probably like to replicate their data on nodes that they trust, and they could be willing to help disseminate content coming primarily from the set of users they trust most, given that untrusted users could be sources of unwanted content such as spammers or bots. Based on these remarks, and on the idea that people have a limited number of social contacts close to them (i.e. a super support clique), Conti et al. [112] proposed a novel replication scheme for DOSNs based on the selection of a limited number of social contacts for each user to be used as hosts for information replicas. At each time, the scheme selects a maximum of two contacts for each ego network, based on using the contact frequency between the ego and these contacts to estimate trust. The scheme has been tested through simulation on a Facebook dataset containing information about social relationships, and about users' online sessions. The results indicate that the replication scheme reaches a minimum of 90% data availability for users with more than 40 friends. For users with fewer friends, the scheme is not able to provide data availability for all the other nodes in the network, but it provides high availability for the nodes inside the ego network of the users, many of which may be offline at the same time.

**Generative Models of Social Network Graphs**
In Chapter 2, we presented several models for the generation of synthetic social network graphs. We have seen that these models fail to reproduce all the characteristic properties observed in real social networks, in particular, the macro- and micro-level properties of network structure, especially those related to ego networks. The model presented in Section 2.5 is a first attempt toward a convergence between these two levels of social network analysis, and already provides quite good results in that it generates social network graphs showing values of global indices of the network, and ego network properties compatible with those observed in offline social

networks. Nevertheless, we believe that the model performance could be significantly improved if the findings presented in this book about the structure of ego networks in Facebook and Twitter were exploited so as to obtain more representative social network graphs. In particular, including knowledge about tie strength and ego network layers in a generative model of social network graphs would allow us to create an interaction graph of a social network, rather than simply its social graph. This would provide a more representative graph for different types of simulations, for example, for the analysis of information diffusion. In the case of the model presented in [70], and described in Section 2.5, the information about the structure of ego networks that is used by the model concerns the distribution of the size and the tie strength of the ego network layers, but considered only the active network, the sympathy group and the support clique since no information about the other layers was available at the time the model was created. Knowledge about the existence of an inner circle of 1.5 members, and the accurate information about the size, and the contact frequency of the various ego network layers of OSNs, and in particular the affinity layer of ~50 alters, could be used to extend the model, possibly resulting in synthetic interaction graphs with characteristics that are more similar to those observed in real communication data, in particular from the point of view of microscopic properties.

## 6.4 BOOK MILESTONES

In this book, we investigated the structural properties of ego networks in OSNs, with particular attention to Facebook and Twitter. We presented a series of analyses aimed at determining whether features that define offline social networks, such as Dunbar's number and the characteristic hierarchical structure of ego networks, also occur in OSNs. Studies of offline social networks suggest that these structural properties are the product of cognitive and time constraints on the capacity of humans to socialise. Thus, a comparison between the structural properties of online and offline social networks is important for understanding how the use of social media is impacting both on our social behaviour and on our capacity to actively maintain social relationships.

The crucial first step in our analyses was being able to characterise and quantify the importance of a social tie (i.e. tie strength) in OSNs. The results from the analysis of Facebook ego networks suggest that we could estimate tie strength from online communication data obtained from OSNs using the contact frequency between users. This allowed us to reconstruct the ego network graphs in OSNs using large-scale communication datasets from Facebook and Twitter. Analysis of these graphs revealed that the structural properties of ego networks are invariant to the use of specific communication media. In particular, the use of OSNs does not improve our social capacity, and the number of social relationships which we actively maintain online is comparable to those defined by the social brain hypothesis (SBH) in the offline world. Moreover, the hierarchical structure of ego networks found in Facebook and Twitter is very similar to that found offline, in terms of both size and typical contact frequency of the layers. This suggests that the properties of online networks are subject to the same cognitive and time constraints that govern the offline world.

In addition, Facebook and Twitter ego networks show an inner layer formed of one or two alters with unusually strong relationships with the ego – a layer that was not visible in the hierarchical structure of ego networks in offline social networks, most likely because the data available from these studies on interaction frequencies were not sufficiently fine-tuned. This inner layer, a 'super' support clique, is formed of an average of 1.5 members, perhaps a partner and/or a best friend of the ego, with very high contact frequency. The layer fits perfectly into the hierarchical structure of the ego network model: it is approximately one-third the size of the support clique, in accordance with the scaling ratio of ~3 between the other layers.

Thanks to the availability of data about social relationships in Twitter over a wide temporal window, we have also been able to analyse the dynamic evolution of social relationships and ego networks over time. The results of this analysis revealed that people constantly establish new connections with others, but, due to cognitive and time constraints, they maintain only a limited number of them as active relationships, in accordance with the SBH. This gives rise to churn, or turnover, in the ego networks in which new members brought into the network result in a comparable number of old members leaving. Although this turnover has been already observed in offline ego networks, in OSNs it is much more pronounced. This seems to be the most important consequence of the use of OSNs: even though our social capacity remains limited in OSNs, the speed at which we create and destroy relationships online is much higher than offline, allowing us to adapt rapidly to sudden changes in our social environments.

# REFERENCES

[1] S. Wasserman, K. Faust, Social Network Analysis in the Social and Behavioral Sciences, Cambridge University Press, 1994.

[2] URL http://www.statista.com/statistics/264810/number-of-monthly-active-facebook-users-worldwide/.

[3] URL http://www.statista.com/statistics/282087/number-of-monthly-active-twitter-users/.

[4] M. Conti, S. Das, C. Bisdikian, M. Kumar, L.M. Ni, A. Passarella, et al., Looking ahead in pervasive computing: challenges and opportunities in the era of cyber-physical convergence, Pervasive Mob. Comput. 8 (2012) 2–21, doi:10.1016/j.pmcj.2011.10.001.

[5] R.I.M. Dunbar, The social brain hypothesis and its implications for social evolution, Ann. Hum. Biol. 36 (5) (1998) 562–572, ISSN 1464-5033, doi:10.1080/03014460902960289.

[6] S. Shultz, R.I.M. Dunbar, Bondedness and sociality, Behaviour 147 (7) (2010) 775–803, ISSN 0005-7959, doi:10.1163/000579510X501151.

[7] S. Shultz, R.I.M. Dunbar, Encephalization is not a universal macroevolutionary phenomenon in mammals but is associated with sociality, Pro. Natl Acad. Sci. USA 107 (50) (2010) 21582–21586, ISSN 0027-8424, doi:10.1073/pnas.1005246107.

[8] R.I.M. Dunbar, Brain and behaviour in primate evolution, in: Mind the Gap: Tracing the Origins of Human Universals, 2010, pp. 315–330.

[9] M.E. Newman, Networks: An Introduction, Oxford University Press, 2010, ISBN 0199206651, 9780199206650.

[10] D. Easley, J. Kleinberg, Networks, Crowds, and Markets: Reasoning About a Highly Connected World, 2010, ISBN 9780521195331, URL http://onlinelibrary.wiley.com/doi/10.1111/j.1740-9713.2012.00594.x/abstract.

[11] M.E. Newman, J. Park, Why social networks are different from other types of networks, Phys. Rev. E 68 (3) (2003), doi:10.1103/PhysRevE.68.036122.

[12] B. Bollobás, The evolution of random graphs, Trans. Am. Math. Soc. 286 (1) (1984) 257, ISSN 00029947, doi:10.2307/1999405.

[13] A. Lancichinetti, S. Fortunato, Community detection algorithms: a comparative analysis, Phys. Rev. E 80 (5) (2009) 1–11, ISSN 15393755, doi:10.1103/PhysRevE.80.056117.

[14] S. Fortunato, Community detection in graphs, Phys. Rep. (3–5) (2010) 75–174, doi:http://dx.doi.org/10.1016/j.physrep.2009.11.002.

[15] J. Travers, S. Milgram, An experimental study of the small world problem, Sociometry 32 (4) (1969) 425, ISSN 00380431, doi:10.2307/2786545.

[16] J. Leskovec, E. Horvitz, Planetary-scale views on an instant-messaging network, Tech. Rep., 2007, arXiv:0803.0939v1.

[17] J. Ugander, B. Karrer, L. Backstrom, C. Marlow, The anatomy of the Facebook social graph, arXiv:1111.4503v1 (2011).

[18] S.A. Myers, A. Sharma, P. Gupta, J. Lin, Information network or social network? The structure of the Twitter follow graph, in: WWW '14, ISBN 9781450327459, 2014, pp. 493–498, URL http://dl.acm.org/citation.cfm?id=2576939.

[19] H. Kwak, C. Lee, H. Park, S. Moon, What is Twitter, a social network or a news media?, in: WWW '10, ISBN 9781605587998, 2010, URL http://dl.acm.org/citation.cfm?id=1772751.

[20] G. Magno, G. Comarela, D. Saez-Trumper, M. Cha, V. Almeida, New kid on the block: exploring the Google+ social graph, in: IMC '12, ISBN 9781450317054, 2012, pp. 159–170, URL http://dl.acm.org/citation.cfm?id=2398794.

[21] D.J. Watts, S.H. Strogatz, Collective dynamics of "small-world" networks, Nature 393 (6684) (1998) 440–442, ISSN 0028-0836, doi:10.1038/30918.

[22] A. Mislove, M. Marcon, K.P. Gummadi, P. Druschel, B. Bhattacharjee, Measurement and analysis of online social networks, in: IMC '07, vol. 40, ISBN 9781595939081, ISSN 09538984, 2007, p. 29, doi:10.1145/1298306.1298311.

[23] A.-L. Barabási, R. Albert, Emergence of scaling in random networks, Science 286 (5439) (1999) 509–512, ISSN 00368075, doi:10.1126/science.286.5439.509.

[24] A. Clauset, C.R. Shalizi, M.E. Newman, Power-law distributions in empirical data, arXiv (2009) ISSN 01403664, doi:10.1109/ICPC.2008.18, URL http://arxiv.org/pdf/0706.1062$\delimiter"026E30F$nhttp://ieeexplore.ieee.org/lpdocs/epic03/wrapper.htm?arnumber=4362913$\delimiter"026E30F$nhttp://www.hpl.hp.com/research/idl/papers/ranking/ranking.html$\delimiter"026E30F$nhttp://ieeexplore.ieee.org/xpls/abs_all.jsp?arnumber=6062085$\delimiter"026E30F$nhttp://ieeexplore.ieee.org.

[25] J.P. Onnela, J. Saramäki, J. Hyvönen, G. Szabó, D. Lazer, K. Kaski, J. Kertész, A.L. Barabási, Structure and tie strengths in mobile communication networks, PNAS 104 (18) (2007) 7332–7336, ISSN 0027-8424, doi:10.1073/pnas.0610245104.

[26] A. Culotta, R. Bekkerman, A. McCallum, Extracting social networks and contact information from email and the Web, in: CEAS '04, 2004.

[27] C. Wilson, A. Sala, K.P. Puttaswamy, B.Y. Zhao, Beyond social graphs: user interactions in online social networks and their implications, ACM Trans. Web 6 (4) (2012) 1–31, ISSN 15591131, doi: 10.1145/2382616.2382620.

[28] D.S. Callaway, M.E. Newman, S.H. Strogatz, D.J. Watts, Network robustness and fragility: percolation on random graphs, Phys. Rev. Lett. 85 (5468) (2000) 1–3, URL http://journals.aps.org/prl/abstract/10.1103/PhysRevLett.85.5468.

[29] M. McPherson, L. Smith-Lovin, J.M. Cook, Homophily in social networks, Ann. Rev. Sociol. 27 (2001) 415–444.

[30] N.A. Christakis, J.H. Fowler, The spread of obesity in a social network, N. Engl. J. Med. 357 (18) (2007) 1866–1867, ISSN 0028-4793, doi:10.1056/NEJMc072478.

[31] N.A. Christakis, J.H. Fowler, Connected: The Surprising Power of Our Social Networks and How They Shape Our Lives, Little, Brown and Company, Hachette Book Group, New York, 2009.

[32] K. Lewis, M. Gonzalez, J. Kaufman, Social selection and peer influence in an online social network, in: PNAS, vol. 109, ISBN 1109739109, ISSN 1091-6490, 2012, pp. 68–72, doi:10.1073/pnas.1109739109, URL http://www.pubmedcentral.nih.gov/articlerender.fcgi?artid=3252911&tool=pmcentrez&rendertype=abstract.

[33] Y. Volkovich, S. Scellato, D. Laniado, C. Mascolo, A. Kaltenbrunner, The length of bridge ties: structural and geographic properties of online social interactions, in: ICWSM '12, 2012.

[34] P.A. Grabowicz, J.J. Ramasco, B. Gonçalves, V.M. Eguíluz, Entangling mobility and interactions in social media, PLoS ONE 9 (3) (2014) e92196, ISSN 1932-6203, doi:10.1371/journal.pone.0092196.

[35] R. Kumar, J. Novak, A. Tomkins, Structure and Evolution of Online Social Networks, ACM Press, New York, NY, USA, 2006, ISBN 1595933395, 611–617, doi:10.1145/1150402.1150476, URL http://portal.acm.org/citation.cfm?doid=1150402.1150476.

[36] Y.-Y. Ahn, S. Han, H. Kwak, S. Moon, H. Jeong, Analysis of topological characteristics of huge online social networking services, in: WWW '07, 2007, pp. 835–844, ISSN 08963207, URL http://doi.acm.org/10.1145/1242572.1242685.

[37] Z. Chen, P. Liu, X. Wang, Y. Gu, Follow whom? Chinese users have different choice, arXiv preprint (2012), URL http://arxiv.org/abs/1212.0167.

[38] J. Jiang, C. Wilson, X. Wang, P. Huang, W. Sha, Y. Dai, B.Y. Zhao, Understanding latent interactions in online social networks, IMC '10 (2010) 369, ISSN 15591131, doi:10.1145/1879141.1879190, URL http://portal.acm.org/citation.cfm?doid=1879141.1879190.

[39] M.E. Newman, Coauthorship networks and patterns of scientific collaboration, PNAS 101 (2004) 5200–5205, ISSN 0027-8424, doi:10.1073/pnas.0307545100.

[40] M.E. Newman, S. Forrest, J. Balthrop, Email networks and the spread of computer viruses, Phys. Rev. E Stat. Nonlinear Soft Matter Phys. 66 (3) (2002) 17–20, ISSN 15393755, doi:10.1103/PhysRevE.66.035101.

[41] A. Broder, R. Kumar, F. Maghoul, P. Raghavan, S. Rajagopalan, R. Stata, A. Tomkins, J. Wiener, Graph structure in the Web, Comput. Commun. 33 (1) (2000) 1–15, ISSN 13891286.

[42] M. Faloutsos, P. Faloutsos, C. Faloutsos, On power-law relationships on the Internet topology, in: Sigcomm '99, 1999.

[43] P. Erdös, A. Rényi, On the evolution of random graphs, PMIHAS 6 (1959) 290–297.

[44] N.Z. Gong, W. Xu, L. Huang, P. Mittal, E. Stefanov, V. Sekar, D. Song, Evolution of social-attribute networks: measurements, modeling, and implications using Google+, in: IMC '12, ISBN 9781450317054, 2012, pp. 131–144.

[45] M.S. Granovetter, The strength of weak ties, Am. J. Sociol. 78 (6) (1973) 1360–1380, doi:10.2307/2776392.

[46] P. Klimek, S. Thurner, Triadic closure dynamics drives scaling laws in social multiplex networks, New J. Phys. 15 (6) (2013) ISSN 1367-2630, doi:10.1088/1367-2630/15/6/063008, URL http://stacks.iop.org/1367-2630/15/i=6/a=063008?key=crossref.0e56147ae7112f371cd58a5c8cc5b4cf.

[47] D. Krackhardt, The ties that torture: simmelian tie analysis in organizations, Res. Sociol. Organ. 16 (1999) 183–210, URL http://www.bebr.ufl.edu/sites/default/files/TheTiesthatTorture-SimmelianTieAnalysisinOrganizations.pdf.

[48] M. Tortoriello, D. Krackhardt, Activating cross-boundary knowledge: the role of simmelian ties in the generation of innovations, Acad. Manag. J 53 (1) (2010) 167–181, ISSN 0001-4273, doi:10.5465/AMJ.2010.48037420, URL http://amj.aom.org/cgi/doi/10.5465/AMJ.2010.48037420.

[49] D. Dekker, Measures of simmelian tie strength, simmelian brokerage, and the simmelianly brokered, J. Soci. Struct. 7 (2006) 1–22, ISSN 15291227.

[50] P.V. Marsden, K.E. Campbell, Measuring tie strength, Soc. Forces 63 (2) (1984) 482–501, doi:10.2307/2579058.

[51] R.I.M. Dunbar, The social brain hypothesis, Evol. Anthropol. 6 (5) (1998) 178–190, doi:10.1002/(SICI)1520-6505(1998)6:5<178::AID-EVAN5>3.0.CO;2-8.

[52] R.I.M. Dunbar, Neocortex size and group size in primates: a test of the hypothesis, J. Hum. Evol. (1995) URL http://www.sciencedirect.com/science/article/pii/S0047248485710214.

[53] R. Kanai, B. Bahrami, R. Roylance, G. Rees, Online social network size is reflected in human brain structure, Biol. Sci. 279 (1732) (2012) 1327–1334, ISSN 1471-2954, doi:10.1098/rspb.2011.1959.

[54] P.A. Lewis, R. Rezaie, R. Brown, N. Roberts, R.I.M. Dunbar, Ventromedial prefrontal volume predicts understanding of others and social network size, NeuroImage 57 (4) (2011) 1624–1629, ISSN 1095-9572, doi:10.1016/j.neuroimage.2011.05.030.

[55] J. Powell, P.A. Lewis, N. Roberts, M. Garcia-Finana, R.I.M. Dunbar, Orbital prefrontal cortex volume predicts social network size: an imaging study of individual differences in humans, Proc. R. Soc. B Biol. Sci. 279 (1736) (2012) 2157–2162.

[56] J.L. Powell, G.J. Kemp, R.I.M. Dunbar, N. Roberts, V. Sluming, M. García-Fi nana, Different association between intentionality competence and prefrontal volume in left- and right-handers, Cortex 54 (1) (2014) 63–76.

[57] J. Sallet, R.B. Mars, M.P. Noonan, J.L. Andersson, J.X. O'Reilly, S. Jbabdi, P.L. Croxson, M. Jenkinson, K.L. Miller, M.F. Rushworth, Social network size affects neural circuits in macaques, 2011.

[58] W.X. Zhou, D. Sornette, R.A. Hill, R.I.M. Dunbar, Discrete hierarchical organization of social group sizes, Biol. Sci. 272 (1561) (2005) 439–444, ISSN 0962-8452, doi:10.1098/rspb.2004. 2970.

[59] R.I.M. Dunbar, Constraints on the evolution of social institutions and their implications for information flow, J. Inst. Econ. 7 (2011) 345–371, ISSN 1744-1374, doi:10.1017/ S1744137410000366.

[60] B. Gonçalves, N. Perra, A. Vespignani, Modeling users' activity on Twitter networks: validation of Dunbar's number, PLoS ONE 6 (8) (2011) e22656, ISSN 1932-6203, doi:10.1371/journal. pone.0022656.

[61] A. Sutcliffe, R.I.M. Dunbar, J. Binder, H. Arrow, Relationships and the social brain: integrating psychological and evolutionary perspectives, Br. J. Psychol. 103 (2) (2012) 149–168, ISSN 0007-1269, doi:10.1111/j.2044-8295.2011.02061.x.

[62] S.G. Roberts, Constraints on social networks, in: Social Brain, Distributed Mind (Proceedings of the British Academy), 2010, pp. 115–134, doi:10.5871/bacad/9780197264522.001.0001.

[63] S.G. Roberts, R.I.M. Dunbar, T.V. Pollet, T. Kuppens, Exploring variation in active network size: constraints and ego characteristics, Soc. Netw. 31 (2) (2009) 138–146, ISSN 03788733, doi:10. 1016/j.socnet.2008.12.002.

[64] R.A. Hill, R.I.M. Dunbar, Social network size in humans, Hum. Nat. 14 (1) (2003) 53–72, ISSN 1045-6767, doi:10.1007/s12110-003-1016-y.

[65] M.J. Hamilton, B.T. Milne, R.S. Walker, O. Burger, J.H. Brown, The complex structure of hunter-gatherer social networks, Biol. Sci. 274 (July) (2007) 2195–2202, ISSN 0962-8452, doi:10.1098/ rspb.2007.0564.

[66] R.A. Hill, A.R. Bentley, R.I.M. Dunbar, Network scaling reveals consistent fractal pattern in hierarchical mammalian societies, Biol. Lett. 4 (6) (2008) 748–751, ISSN 1744-9561, doi:10. 1098/rsbl.2008.0393.

[67] R.I.M. Dunbar, M. Spoors, Social networks, support cliques and kinship, Hum. Nat. 6 (3) (1995) 273–290.

[68] R.S. Burt, Structural holes versus network closure as social capital, in: Social Capital: Theory and Research, 2001, pp. 31–56.

[69] D. Quercia, L. Capra, J. Crowcroft, The social world of Twitter: topics, geography, and emotions, in: ICWSM '12, 2012.

[70] M. Conti, A. Passarella, F. Pezzoni, A model to represent human social relationships in social network graphs, in: Social Informatics, 2012, URL http://link.springer.com/chapter/10.1007/978-3-642-35386-4_14.

[71] I. Jolliffe, Principal component analysis, Technometrics 30 (3) (2002) 487, ISSN 00401706, doi: 10.2307/1270093, URL http://onlinelibrary.wiley.com/doi/10.1002/0470013192.bsa501/full.

[72] E. Gilbert, K. Karahalios, Predicting tie strength with social media, in: CHI '09, ISBN 9781605582467, 2009, pp. 211–220.

[73]  E. Gilbert, Predicting tie strength in a new medium, in: CSCW '12, ISBN 9781450310864, 2012, pp. 1047–1056.

[74]  H. Khosravi, A. Bozorgkhan, O. Schulte, Transaction-based link strength prediction in a social network, in: CIDM '13, ISBN 9781467358958, 2013, pp. 191–198, URL http://www.cs.sfu.ca/oschulte/files/pubs/cidm-friendship.pdf.

[75]  R. Xiang, J. Neville, M. Rogati, Modeling relationship strength in online social networks, in: WWW '10, 2010, pp. 1–8.

[76]  J.J. Jones, J.E. Settle, R.M. Bond, C.J. Fariss, C. Marlow, J.H. Fowler, Inferring tie strength from online directed behavior, PLoS ONE 8 (1) (2013) e52168, ISSN 1932-6203, doi:10.1371/journal.pone.0052168.

[77]  A. Wu, J.M. DiMicco, D.R. Millen, Detecting professional versus personal closeness using an enterprise social network site, in: CHI '10, ISBN 9781605589299, 2010, pp. 1955, doi:10.1145/1753326.1753622, URL http://portal.acm.org/citation.cfm?doid=1753326.1753622.

[78]  V. Arnaboldi, A. Guazzini, A. Passarella, Egocentric online social networks: analysis of key features and prediction of tie strength in Facebook, Comput. Commun. 36 (10–11) (2013) 1130–1144, ISSN 0140-3664, doi:10.1016/j.comcom.2013.03.003.

[79]  V. Arnaboldi, A. Passarella, M. Tesconi, D. Gazzè, Towards a characterization of egocentric networks in online social networks, in: OTM Workshops, vol. 7046, ISBN 978-3-642-25125-2, 2011, pp. 524–533.

[80]  M.L. Gala, V. Arnaboldi, A. Passarella, M. Conti, Ego-net Digger: a new way to study ego networks in online social networks, in: KDD Workshops, ISBN 9781450315494, 2012, pp. 9–16.

[81]  URL http://overstated.net/2009/03/09/maintained-relationships-on-facebook, 2009.

[82]  V. Arnaboldi, M. Conti, A. Passarella, F. Pezzoni, Analysis of ego network structure in online social networks, in: SocialCom '12, 2012, pp. 31–40.

[83]  R.I.M. Dunbar, V. Arnaboldi, M. Conti, A. Passarella, The structure of online social networks mirrors those in the offline world, Soc. Netw. 43 (2015) 39–47, ISSN 03788733, doi:10.1016/j.socnet.2015.04.005.

[84]  URL http://current.cs.ucsb.edu/facebook.

[85]  B. Viswanath, A. Mislove, M. Cha, K.P. Gummadi, On the evolution of user interaction in Facebook, in: WOSN, ISBN 9781605584454, 2009, pp. 37–42.

[86]  H. Wang, M. Song, Clustering in one dimension by dynamic programming, R J. 3 (2) (2011) 29–33.

[87]  H. Akaike, A new look at the statistical model identification, IEEE Trans. Autom. Control 19 (6) (1974) 716–723, ISSN 00189286, doi:10.1109/TAC.1974.1100705, URL http://ieeexplore.ieee.org/lpdocs/epic03/wrapper.htm?arnumber=1100705.

[88]  H.P. Kriegel, P. Kröger, J. Sander, A. Zimek, Density-based clustering, Data Min. Knowl. Disc. 1 (3) (2011) 231–240.

[89]  M. Ester, H.P. Kriegel, J. Sander, X. Xu, A density-based algorithm for discovering clusters in large spatial databases with noise, in: KDD, 1996, pp. 226–231.

[90]  V. Arnaboldi, M. Conti, A. Passarella, F. Pezzoni, Ego networks in Twitter: an experimental analysis, in: NetSciCom '13, 2013, pp. 3459–3464.

[91]  M. Muller, D.R. Millen, S.N. Shami, J. Feinberg, We are all Lurkers: toward a Lurker research agenda, in: CSCW '10, 2010, pp. 1–10.

[92]  M. De Choudhury, N. Diakopoulos, M. Naaman, Unfolding the event landscape on Twitter: classification and exploration of user categories, in: CSCW '12, 2012, pp. 241–244, URL http://dl.acm.org/citation.cfm?id=2145242.

[93]  C. Cortes, V. Vapnik, Support-vector networks, Mach. Learn. 20 (3) (1995) 273–297, doi:10. 1023/A:1022627411411.

[94]  C. Aggarwal, K. Subbian, Evolutionary network analysis: a survey, ACM Comput. Surv. 47 (1) (2014) 1–36.

[95]  X. Zhao, A. Sala, C. Wilson, X. Wang, S. Gaito, H. Zheng, B.Y. Zhao, Multi-scale dynamics in a massive online social network, in: IMC '12, ISBN 9781450317054, 2012, pp. 171–184.

[96]  G. Miritello, R. Lara, M. Cebrian, E. Moro, Limited communication capacity unveils strategies for human interaction, Sci. Rep. 3 (2013) 1–7, ISSN 2045-2322, doi:10.1038/srep01950, URL http://www.nature.com/doifinder/10.1038/srep01950.

[97]  J. Saramäki, E.A. Leicht, E. Lopez, S.G. Roberts, F. Reed-Tsochas, R.I.M. Dunbar, The persistence of social signatures in human communication, PNAS 111 (3) (2014) 942–947.

[98]  G. Miritello, E. Moro, R. Lara, Time as a limited resource: communication strategy in mobile phone networks, arXiv preprint, 2013, URL http://arxiv.org/abs/1301.2464.

[99]  M. Sweney, Facebook sees first dip in UK users – guardian.co.uk, 2008, URL http://www. guardian.co.uk.

[100] Y.E. Lu, S. Roberts, P. Lio, R.I.M. Dunbar, J. Crowcroft, Size matters: variation in personal network size, personality and effect on information transmission, in: CSE '09, 2009, URL http:// ieeexplore.ieee.org/xpls/abs_all.jsp?arnumber=5284189.

[101] E. Bakshy, I. Rosenn, C. Marlow, L. Adamic, The role of social networks in information diffusion, in: WWW '12, ISBN 9781450312295, 2012, pp. 519–528.

[102] S. Myers, C. Zhu, J. Leskovec, Information diffusion and external influence in networks, in: SIGKDD '12, ISBN 9781450314626, 2012, arXiv:1206.1331v1.

[103] M. Cha, A. Mislove, K.P. Gummadi, A Measurement-Driven Analysis of Information Propagation in the Flickr Social Network, ACM Press, New York, NY, USA, ISBN 9781605584874, 721 doi: 10.1145/1526709.1526806.

[104] V. Arnaboldi, M. Conti, M. La Gala, A. Passarella, F. Pezzoni, Information diffusion in OSNs: the impact of nodes' sociality, in: SAC '14, ISBN 9781450324694, 2014, pp. 1–6.

[105] V. Arnaboldi, M.L. La Gala, A. Passarella, M. Conti, The role of trusted relationships on content spread in distributed online social networks, in: LSDVE '14, 2014, pp. 287–298.

[106] Diaspora Project, URL https://diasporafoundation.org/.

[107] S. Buchegger, D. Schioberg, L.H. Vu, A. Datta, PeerSoN: P2P social networking – early experiences and insights, in: SocialNets '09, ISBN 9781605584638, 2009, pp. 46–52.

[108] L.A. Cutillo, R. Molva, T. Strufe, Safebook: a privacy-preserving online social network leveraging on real-life trust, IEEE Commun. Mag. 47 (12) (2009) 94–101.

[109] T. Paul, A. Famulari, T. Strufe, A survey on decentralized online social networks, Comput. Netw. 75 (2014) 437–452, ISSN 13891286, doi:10.1016/j.comnet.2014.10.005.

[110] L. Han, B. Nath, L. Iftode, S. Muthukrishnan, Social butterfly: social caches for distributed social networks, in: SocialCom '11, ISBN 978-1-4577-1931-8, 2011, pp. 81–86, doi:10.1109/PASSAT/ SocialCom.2011.105.

[111] F. Xia, A. Ahmed, L. Yang, J. Ma, J. Rodrigues, Exploiting social relationship to enable efficient replica allocation in ad-hoc social networks, IEEE Trans. Parallel Distrib. Syst. (2013) 1–11, ISSN 1045-9219, doi:10.1109/TPDS.2013.2295805.

[112] M. Conti, A. De Salve, B. Guidi, F. Pitto, L. Ricci, Trusted dynamic storage for Dunbar-based P2P online social networks, in: OTM '14, 2014, pp. 400–417.

Printed in the United States
By Bookmasters